# RAISING CHILDREN WITH CHRONIC ILLNESS

## *A Mother's Journey*

Dana P. Rogers Ph.D RN

ISBN 978-1-64468-130-5 (Paperback)
ISBN 978-1-64468-131-2 (Digital)

Covenant Books, Inc.
11661 Hwy 707
Murrells Inlet, SC 29576
www.covenantbooks.com

# Preface

In more than thirty years of work in healthcare as both a licensed psychologist and registered nurse, I have watched many parents care for children who have a chronic illness. I have always marveled at those parents who seemed to somehow manage to make things "okay" for their child in adjusting to their specific health problem. I never thought that one day I would be one of those parents who diligently tried to make things "okay" for my children who were diagnosed with chronic illnesses.

I am often asked what coping strategies helped me in raising two children with significant health problems. I initially took pause with this question but then realized there actually were some specific things that helped me cope with the health problems that faced both of my children. This became the impetus for writing this book. I hope that by sharing my journey it may be of some benefit to other parents struggling to cope with their child's illness.

# The Joy of Childbirth, or Is It?

Isn't giving birth to a newborn child supposed to be a joyous, wonderful, and positive experience? Usually the answer to that question is an unequivocal yes. But when there is something wrong with that newborn infant, emotions of fear and sadness can overshadow the immediate joy of giving birth. This happened to me with the birth of both of my children. At birth, both children had life threatening physical conditions requiring immediate medical care. Baker, my oldest son, had serious breathing problems and had to be put on a respirator because of hyaline membrane disease (not enough surfactant in the lungs to keep tiny air sacs open) and a patent ductus arteriosus (a hole between the right and left side of the heart that had not yet closed). My husband and I were told that this condition resulted from Baker's prematurity. He was on a respirator for well over a week. He was discharged after two weeks in the hospital. Much later in childhood, another serious illness surfaced for Baker.

Our second son, Jason, needed intestinal surgery within twenty-four hours after his birth because of cystic fibrosis. Cystic fibrosis (CF) is a genetic disease that affects the lungs and gastrointestinal tract with thick, concentrated sticky mucous. At birth Jason had a blockage in his small intestine called meconium ileus (stool that is sticky like tar in the ileum section of the small intestine). This blockage required immediate intestinal surgery resulting in a ten-week stay in the neonatal intensive care unit before he was able to come home.

# Finding Meaning and Purpose

I don't know why bad things happen to good people, especially when those people are newborn children. It is not my goal in life to figure that out. I believe that question can be answered only by the higher power of God. But the older I get, the more often I see that bad things do sometimes happen to children that you just can't explain. As a psychologist and registered nurse, I have dealt with many families who have been faced with difficult psychiatric or physical problems that their children face at various times in their lives. For me, both children were faced with serious health challenges. Why did both my children have to endure suffering with health problems? I don't know. Even to this day I still don't know. I have come to the realization that I will probably never know!

What happens when your child gets a bad diagnosis? It could be physical, like cancer or a brain tumor, or genetic like cystic fibrosis, or sickle cell anemia. Your child gets a diagnosis like that and your world suddenly comes to a dead stop. Your dreams of that child's future are put in question. How long will they live? What will they be able to do? How will they cope? And yes, how will you cope and adapt to the limitations your child may have to face? The whole family will be affected in some way by your child's illness. Don't kid yourself that it won't. A serious illness of one family member impacts all family members to some degree.

Don't let what you are told about your child's illness discourage you. For example, we were told by Jason's physician that Jason had a severe case of cystic fibrosis and would probably only live to be ten years of age. He is now thirty years old. It has not been easy for Jason to get to this age of thirty. It took a liver transplant and later a double lung transplant to get there. However, he managed to finish two college degrees after his lung transplant, and he works as an RN in psychiatric nursing. He lives independently with his golden retriever dog Berkley. For Baker, after his initial breathing trouble at birth, he later had a terrible virus that basically tore up the tissue in his colon and required a complete colectomy. Since that very difficult time in Baker's life, he has gone on to get an undergraduate and graduate degree in a science/medical field. He just recently bought a new house, just got engaged, and has a brand new puppy. Even at a young age, both boys have always shown significant perseverance in what medical challenges faced them.

I like the motto I recently read on top of a baseball cap, "Scars are the new tattoo with a better story." This motto applies to my young men. They have experienced quite a lot of trauma with their illnesses. When they pull up their shirts you can see the scar history, and boy, do they ever have a scar history! But the victories they have achieved are what is most important to me. They are two very resilient young men. Overcoming difficulties and adversity in life is what helps to build resilience.

Your child's limitations may be such that any vocational and academic achievement is quite difficult. Finding something meaningful to occupy your child's time, and enhance self-esteem, and encourage independence is an important goal to try to achieve. We have friends who have children with intellectual disabilities. The parent's creativity in finding things their children can do to help with esteem building and self-confidence is wonderful to see. Tapping into local community resources that support and serve people with similar diagnoses as your child may be quite helpful to you. We stayed connected with the local CF chapter in our city for Jason and ulcerative colitis organization for Baker. We made some very meaningful connections with other families in these two organizations. Jason and Baker remember a couple of fun field trip outings they attended through their respective organization.

Yes, there are difficult and sad times in raising a child with physical, mental or emotional limitations. But there are some amazing and wonderful times as well. The joys of watching them accomplish things, even with their challenges, can warm a parent's heart with joy and pride. I tried to help each boy maximize his potential. Illness can create family dysfunction and stress, but it can also bring a family closer together and unite them around that members special needs. I have witnessed this in my practice as a psychologist and in my own family. Being a strong advocate for your child every step of the way is critical. Never lose this focus. I believe every individual's life has purpose and meaning no matter how altered one's life may be. As parents, we are the anchor our child so desperately holds on to when turbulent waters of disease and illness threaten to overtake them.

I really love the psychiatrist Viktor Frankl who wrote the book *Man's Search for Meaning*. I have read it before and pulled it out two or three times during rough times in my boys' illnesses. To date it is still referenced by many other clinicians who have adapted his work. In his book, Frankl writes about his experience in Nazi concentration camps. He explained how prisoners of war who were relentlessly tortured survived by finding meaning and purpose to their very existence. He went on to develop logotherapy. Logotherapy focuses on helping individuals find meaning in their lives and encourages them to look to the future. At times, the suffering I watched my children experience seemed relentless. So many times, I wished I could take their place and endure the suffering they were experiencing. Most any parent would gladly switch places if they could. Parent stability and parental encouragement are critical for the child during these times. I encourage parents to rally their personal support system so they can stay strong for their child during these very difficult times of pain and suffering.

As a psychologist, I help people solve problems for a living. A basic premise of positive psychology is that hope and optimism are central in overcoming difficulties. I claimed these in raising my children. I believe that it is not only what happens to us in life that is important, but also our perspective and response to what happens to us. Our perspective on what we are experiencing affects our adaptation in times of difficulty. I believe it is possible to be realistic and also hopeful about your child's illness at the same time, even during the tough times. I claimed this in my journey with both children's health problems.

# Getting Centered with What Was Happening

Each time, after getting Baker's diagnosis and later Jason's, I tried to make sense out of what was happening. I asked myself, "What am I supposed to learn from this journey I am being forced to travel?" Every step of the way I worked hard to get the best medical care I could find. I had to be able to communicate well with the physicians and feel that they valued my concerns and answered my questions clearly. Parents, I encourage you to do the same. Learn as much as you can about your child's illness and what to expect. The more informed you can be, the better equipped you will be to make good health care choices for your child. Let the medical professionals, family, friends, and all possible support resources help you. You will come to dearly value these support resources when times are tough.

Along with caring for a sick child it is easy to forget your own physical and emotional needs. Parents tend to always want to put their child first. I fully understand this as a parent, but this health journey with your child may be like a marathon. That is what it was like for me anyway. You don't want to deplete your personal resources too early in the race and not make it to the finish line. Your child will be depending on you to see them through. Remember, it may be hard for you to care for your child when your emotional and physical resources are depleted. Please pay attention to your own personal health. So now, let me share with you my journey is raising my children with chronic illnesses.

# My Pregnancy and Delivery with Baker

With each pregnancy I had to go on some degree of bedrest because of preterm labor contractions. I remember my trips to the OB doctor and the weigh ins and finger sticks. I hated those finger sticks and I didn't like the weigh-ins either. I remember, after several visits with the OB group, I had my first visit with Dr. Sue. She had recently joined the OB practice and had three children herself. I liked seeing a female who had experienced what I was going through. I had an unusually good connection with Dr. Sue right off the bat. Over time, we developed a wonderful professional relationship and became friends outside the practice. At the time of my first visit with her, I was already dilated and having some contractions. I was just six months into the pregnancy. She suggested that I go home, prop my feet up, and order Chinese takeout. That sounded good to me and I really liked Chinese any way. For about a month, I was on bedrest and taking it easy. At eight months my water broke. I immediately called the OB practice and was instructed to go to the hospital. I remember the OB/GYN telling me the baby would do much better on the outside than trying to stay on the inside. I called my husband and he rushed home from work. Off we went to the hospital. It was a fast trip! We made it to the hospital in record time, but I stayed in labor for over twenty-four hours. I was given a drug called Pitocin IV to speed up my labor contractions. Quickly the contractions started coming with an intensity that was most unpleasant. I think I said a few expletives along the way. I remember getting very irritated looking over at my husband on a cot trying to sleep during all this. I mean really, "How could he do that?" It was only three am and we had been at the hospital for eighteen hours by then. I think men must have some type of innate capacity to block things out around them when they need to sleep and recharge. I have always wished I was better at that. Anyway, I would wake him a few times to push on my back with a tennis ball. This was supposed to help relieve some of the back pain associated with labor contractions. This is what we were taught in the delivery class. "Good God," I thought, "couldn't he press any harder?" There was nothing he could do to comfort me, and this just irritated me more. I was tired, hungry, irritated and in pain. Mothers, I think you can get a visual of my emotional state at that time.

The oldest member of the OB/GYN practice was the physician on call that night. He was calming and reassuring and that immediately put me at ease. On his direction I gave one final push and out came Baker. The medical professionals involved with the delivery were all quickly alerted to Baker's difficulty breathing. He was immediately taken to the neonatal intensive care unit of the hospital. All I saw of him was a thick head of dark hair as he was swaddled up in a blanket and rushed out of my sight. I never got to touch or hold him. Baker weighed a little less than six pounds. We did not expect to have a big baby, but we did anticipate having a healthy baby.

I quickly reviewed thoughts about my pregnancy that came flooding into the forefront of my mind. Why was this happening? I did everything I knew to do to have a healthy pregnancy and baby. I read tons of books on the subject. I kept a healthy weight. I swam often during my pregnancy. I focused on good nutrition and took prenatal vitamins. I even listened to relaxing music and read to my baby in the womb. I had felt wonderful during my pregnancy, except for some early contractions. It was hard to make sense out of what was happening. Everything was moving so quickly. I was caught up in a whirlwind quite unfamiliar to me.

Baker was immediately put on a respirator with positive airway pressure. This was to keep the tiny air sacs in his lungs fully expanded. He had several IVs delivering medicine to him at the time I was wheeled around to see him in the neonatal intensive care unit. The respirator was still in use and critical at that time to support his proper breathing. He was given a medicine called Indocin to close his patent ductus arteriosus. This medicine had just started being used to close the hole between the two chambers of the heart that most frequently resulted from prematurity. The neonatologist told us that just a couple of months earlier, Indocin had been approved for closing a patent ductus. Otherwise open-heart surgery would have been the only way to close the hole between the two chambers of his heart. Fortunately, we skated by this one. It was such a huge relief to know that Baker did not need this surgery. We were relieved when the neonatologist told us that the Indocin had been successful. Thank goodness, no open-heart surgery was needed.

Baker was on a respirator for several days. I remember this quite vividly because I could not hold him until he was off the respirator. My first nursing job had been working in a neonatal intensive care unit. Numerous times I had to suction the lungs of premature infants on respirators. I was accustomed to this scene with other people's children, but watching my son being suctioned by a nurse brought tears to my eyes. I could see he was crying but I could not hear him because of the endotracheal tube in his throat. There was nothing I could do to comfort him. I had suctioned premature infants with hyaline membrane disease many times, but when it was my child, it was a totally different animal of emotion.

I also remember the unpleasant encounter with a very pushy, young neonatologist. Every time I saw him, he quizzed me on what my pregnancy was like, and what medicines I had taken. It felt like he asked me twenty million questions. A little exaggeration here, but that is what it felt like. I kept telling him I had not taken any medications during pregnancy. Didn't he believe me? So one day, I bowed up at this doctor. Was he suggesting that I had done something to cause this scenario? By this point I was emotionally exhausted and physically uncomfortable from a large episiotomy. I had not slept in well over twenty-four hours. However, the doctor's questions kept coming. I was starting to get very irritated. No, I was fuming! The neonatologist stepped back a little with me and tried to explain his line of questioning. He said that only one out of one hundred infants would have hyaline membrane disease at eight months, and he was trying to evaluate if there was a specific contributing factor.

However, his questioning made me question myself and wonder if I was responsible for Baker's illness. I never did like that neonatologist after that encounter. He needed better therapeutic communication skills. In layman's terms his bedside manner stunk!

Seven days after Baker was born, I finally got to hold him and feed him. I had waited thirty-three years to have a child and being able to hold and feed my child was a most rewarding and fulfilling experience. I think I was exploding with love at that moment. Mothers you know what I am talking about. It is a unique bond like no other love relationship.

I had to leave the hospital without Baker and that was very disappointing. Every day that I came to see him in the neonatal intensive care unit, I had to walk by the rooms of mothers with their healthy babies. Well, that just stunk. I wasn't sure yet when Baker would get to come home, but I was more than ready. Each day I came to the hospital I would bring my ice chest filled with breast milk. My poor husband had to listen to that breast pump machine in the middle of the night when I would have to pump. He had a nick name for the breast-pump, but I won't tell you that one.

My visits continued for two weeks. Each day I had to walk through the halls with the new mothers and their healthy babies. I had so much wanted this to be my scenario. Finally, the day came when I got to bring Baker home. Hallelujah, what a glorious day! Chase, Baker and I were finally riding home together in the car! My family of three was now all together. I don't remember how many pictures we took that day, but I know it was quite a lot. Neighbors and family came a day or two later to see our cute little guy. I was somewhat "over the top" by insisting on extremely good handwashing for anyone wanting to hold him. After all, he did have a tough start, and the nurses did emphasize being extra careful.

I marveled over this child. I spent hours watching him sleep and breath. I know, other mothers told me to catch as much sleep as I could when the baby would sleep. This was hard for me to do because I was mesmerized by this new life. At age thirty-three I was a first-time mom, and boy was I proud. I waited a long time to be a mother. I was one of these people who had to do things in order. For example, the month I passed the oral and final part of my psychology licensing exam I found out I was pregnant with Baker. I also had my career solid before children which was a blessing because of all the medical bills we incurred. Medical bills were huge and at times a painful reality.

Four weeks after Baker was born, I went back to work seeing a few clients for psychotherapy in the evenings. My husband would come in from work and I would head out for a few sessions with clients. The office was close to my home which was very convenient. My mother and mother-in-law also volunteered to care for Baker when I worked. As Baker grew older, I was able to increase my work schedule to four days a week. At this stage, I found home care, but this lasted only a few months. After many unsuccessful attempts at home care, I took Baker to daycare at the church where my mother-in-law worked in one of the pastor's office. She could check on him during the day while I was at work. If there was ever a problem with Baker, she could call me and let me know. This was a big comfort, especially for a new mom.

The daycare at the church worked well for Baker. Around this time, I began running again. When I would go running, I would outfit Baker in Nike running shoes just like mine and take him along. I would go jogging with him buckled securely in a running type-stroller and push him along as I ran. People from church would often see us running. He got a cute nickname from the ladies in the church nursery. When I would drop him off at the nursery, he became known as the "The JOGGER." This name stuck with him for several years. Other mothers often asked me why I ran. I would politely reply that it was my therapy. It was a great way for me to destress and get those mood elevating brain chemicals flowing. It was and still is a lot cheaper than professional therapy too. Take my word for it!

I think a special challenge for parents of children with chronic illness is that never-ending battle of finding the right kind of care, especially when both parents work. Most parents have to work to keep insurance, have other children at home to care for, or simply needed to work to pay for the mounting medical bills they have acquired or anticipate acquiring. Extended hospital stays and surgical procedures can be quite expensive. Also, parent's sick leave may have been used up by the lengthy stay in the hospital or from extended bedrest before the actual delivery.

So for over a year and six months, my family of three were rocking along in-sync. Baker, Chase and I had developed a smooth schedule around working and childcare. Then, at age thirty-five, I became pregnant with our second child Jason. I had absolutely no problem with my second pregnancy until early dilation, contractions, and spotting started. Up until that time, I felt terrific. I was working, eating healthy, taking prenatal vitamins, and gently swimming in the pool for exercise. I had a ton of energy and felt great! I was engaged in some typical nesting behavior as most mothers do in preparation for a new baby. The nursery was all tidied up and the house was in tip top shape. We were ready for our new family addition. We had great anticipation for the next baby and planned for a smooth delivery.

# My Pregnancy and Delivery with Jason

When an expectant mother is thirty-five years of age, OB/GYN doctors typically bring up the subject of an amniocentesis. My husband and I talked about this, and we decided to go ahead with it in preparation for what may follow. I have always done better when I knew what to expect. If I had to face difficulties I wanted to know. The amniocentesis report was good. However, at that time cystic fibrosis was not routinely checked. There was no reason to check for it because there was no family history of CF in either of our families. I was told, by my OB/GYN, that except for the CF gene not tested, we could expect a healthy baby. All I heard was I was going to have a healthy baby. I thought, alright, let's do this thing!

At eleven weeks before my due date, I had some preterm labor contractions, spotting and dilation. I went to the OB/GYN office. I was immediately ordered to stay in bed except to go to the bathroom. This was scary stuff! I had another child to take care of and a job as a psychologist at a local hospital. The OB/GYN told me she had to go on strict bed-rest herself when she was pregnant, and I had to also. She meant business and I listened to what she had to say. So as a mom, I was determined to stay on strict bedrest as ordered for eleven weeks. I was going to do everything I could for this baby to have an easy start. I would not take any chances because I wanted my next delivery to be smooth and easy for this baby.

The OB/GYN put me on a home uterine contraction monitor to closely observe contractions throughout my bed rest. I would have frequent conversations on the phone with the nurses who monitored my number of contractions per hour. If I had too many contractions per hour the home health monitoring nurse would call and ask me how I was doing and what I was doing. A highlight to my day of bedrest, while Baker was at daycare and Chase at work, was chatting with these nice nurses on the phone. I got to know several of them on a first name basis and learned just a little about them. I probably asked these nurses too many questions, but I was flat out bored!

The nurses often instructed me to drink lots of fluids to help diminish my contractions. I have never been a good water drinker. Even as a runner I have always chosen other fluids for hydration besides plain water. Gatorade, so I was told, was not a good fluid choice to drink at that time because of sugar and salt content. The nurses suggested that weak decaffeinated tea was a good option since I didn't like water. The decaffeinated tea worked well for me. I also was having to take a drug daily called terbutaline to help slow the contractions of my uterus and prevent preterm labor.

Even after all my efforts at bedrest, drinking large volumes of fluids and taking the medication terbutaline, I had to go to the hospital for preterm labor contractions. I was admitted to the hospital for three days. I had to take magnesium sulfate by IV to avoid early labor. This was truly not a pleasant experience. The magnesium sulfate IV made me feel awful!

My nineteen-month-old child Baker had trouble understanding why I had to stay in bed all day. He wanted me to be up and playing with him. We did a lot of book reading and games we could play together on top of my bed. He adapted as well as he could to the new routine. But this was a big adjustment for both of us. My husband or mother-in-law took Baker to the church daycare center every day now rather than his usual four days a week.

I watched the entire summer go by from my bedroom window. Church friends and neighbors were awesome about bringing meals to the house. My husband is a wonderful husband with many skills, but cooking is not one of them. It seemed like it rained every day that summer. I was kind of glad about that since I could not be outside anyway. I can't tell you how many movies I watched and books I read that summer. I am a high energy level kind of person and extended bedrest was hard for me.

I managed to get to thirty-seven weeks and the terbutaline medicine was stopped by the OB/GYN. I immediately started having intense contractions and off we rushed to the hospital. My next-door neighbor came over to keep Baker until my mother-in-law arrived. Mrs. Carter was the best neighbor any young mother could have. My labor with Jason was quick. By the time we made it to the hospital I was already dilated to a seven out of ten. My favorite OB/GYN, Dr. Sue was on call that day. Chase and I were both happy to see that she would be doing the delivery. I was quite uncomfortable and Dr. Sue ordered an epidural. After the epidural I could focus and enjoy the delivery. I remember her saying "Do you want to push?" I said, "Heck yeah I want to push!" Then out came Jason. I thanked God for that little blessing! Dr. Sue was awesome during the delivery. We were all laughing and joking like we were having a fun private party. This delivery was so neat and so different from my first with Baker's breathing difficulties. After all those weeks of bedrest, I enjoyed every minute of this wonderful delivery!

I remember the first thing my husband said as the delivery was taking place. He said that Jason looked just like Baker! Jason for sure looked very much like Baker did at delivery. He had a very thick head of dark hair just like Baker and was almost the exact same size. I got to hold him right after delivery, which was something I did not get to do with Baker. He was a whopping six pounds and nineteen inches long. Again, he was not a large baby, but neither were the parents. This was just what we expected and hoped for, a healthy baby boy. We began taking a lot of baby pictures and chatted happily together. We enjoyed every minute of this special moment.

After Jason was cleaned up, he was brought to me in my room. I had a few hours with him. He was unusually sleepy and didn't want to take to breast feeding. I remember having the lactation specialist come to my room to check this out. I even remember her name. It was Jana. She wondered, why the baby would not eat? She could find no reason for this. She commented to me that I was doing everything right at that point. Boy, she sure knew just how to affirm a new mother! It is such a natural impulse for newborn babies to take to the mother's breast to feed, but not for Jason.

# Something Is Wrong with Jason

Well, we soon learned why Jason was not breast feeding. The joy of holding him came to an abrupt detour. The pediatrician came to my room and told me that there was something seriously wrong with my child and the surgeon would be coming in shortly to talk with me. I was so taken off guard by these words. I am sure I must have looked stunned and anxious by what I was told. My husband had gone down to the cafeteria to get some lunch, but he quickly returned. The surgeon came as expected and explained to us that Jason had a blockage in his intestine called a meconium ileus and needed immediate surgery. He told us that our son had cystic fibrosis (CF) a genetic disease that affects the lungs and gastrointestinal tract with thick, concentrated sticky mucous. We both looked at each other somewhat bemused and asked which one of us had given it to him. The surgeon explained that we both were carriers of the CF gene. The surgeon went on to explain that the blockage in Jason's small intestine was caused by his cystic fibrosis and needed to be surgically removed. The memory that came flooding into my mind at that very moment was all the cystic fibrosis children I had cared for as a nurse. These children had such gunky lungs filled with mucous that they needed frequent suctioning and ongoing chest therapy to breathe. This was an image I will never forget, and it came rushing to the forefront of my mind at the very moment I heard the words cystic fibrosis. Was this really what my child had? I had to ask myself that question several times before it sunk in. When it did sink in it was overwhelming painful!

The next morning the pediatrician, with whom I had a very good relationship, came by my room and had a heartfelt talk with me. He told me that having a child with cystic fibrosis was going to require all the professional and personal coping strategies I could muster. He also told me, as he gave me a warm hug, that he had faith that I could do this and successfully give Jason what he needed. Boy, was he ever right about using every possible coping strategy I had in raising a child with CF! For so many years, I felt the ups and downs of Jason's illness as if we were riding on a gigantic roller coaster. There were highs and lows that seemed to go on relentlessly. But then there were just a lot of lows…until transplantation.

During the second day of Jason's life, he had intestinal surgery that involved having eight inches of his small intestine removed. When I saw him in the neonatal intensive care unit, he had an ileostomy bag that seemed huge compared to his little body. He also had several other IVs and tubes connected to him. He had nasal cannula oxygen going in his nose. He was going to have to keep his ileostomy bag for eight weeks according to the surgeon, before he could reconnect his small intestine. The surgeon said that the eight-week wait was to avoid unnecessary scar tissue formation that could cause more intestinal blockage. He had to stay in the neonatal intensive care unit during this time. I remember this surgeon so very well and how he stood firm with the neonatologist. The surgeon was adamant that Jason needed the full eight weeks for the intestine to heal before reconnecting it. The chief neonatologist wanted Jason's small intestine to be reconnected sooner for growth reasons, electrolyte balance and other things I don't quite remember. Later in Jason's life we met other parents of CF kids who had the same meconium ileus problem that Jason had. We often heard of their stories of repeated intestinal obstructions after the initial surgery requiring other subsequent intestinal surgeries. We were so thankful for Jason's surgeon being so skilled in his craft.

To add insult to injury, the CF specialist told me during one of my visits with Jason that Baker could have CF, too. She said that CF may have not presented itself yet in Baker, but he had a one in four chance of having it. Well, the odds were not going in our favor. I did not want to open that Pandora's box of trouble. I knew my psyche could not deal with that much stress all at once. I would choose later to have Baker sweat tested to confirm or rule out CF. Sweat testing evaluates the percentage of salt concentration in a child's perspiration. I learned that CF children have high concentrations of salt in their sweat. The CF specialist wanted to know when she could expect to sweat test, Baker? She was adamant that it should be done as soon as possible so if he has CF, she can begin treatment early. I said very firmly that I will test Baker when Jason gets home, and I know Jason will be okay. I could tell she was not happy with my answer.

I thought to myself, now why in the world would she bring this up to me now. I said this because, at that point in time, Baker was extremely healthy. His pediatrician would often comment on Baker's exceptional good health and very muscular physique for a child his age. My husband said for me to take the lead on the decision of when to sweat test Baker. I exerted my sense of control over when this test would be done. It would be after Jason came home from the hospital and I knew that I could manage Jason's health problems myself. I typically don't respond well to ultimatums, and I didn't this time either.

Genetically, with each of us being carriers, there was a one out of four chance that any of our children could have a full-blown case of CF. I knew deep down that Baker could have CF. This was a lot to process as we in the field of counseling would say. I had to give myself time to absorb what was happening. I did what any good mother would probably have done at that time. I took ownership of the things I could control. I could not change the very real possibility that Baker might also have CF. However, I could control when I would let myself come face to face with that possibility.

When one child is very ill and the health of the other child comes into question, this thing called coping takes on a whole new dimension. Compartmentalizing can at times be a healthy coping strategy to prevent flooding of too much painful information all at once. I have even witnessed a few of my client's dissociate (lose touch with reality) when the emotional pain they were experiencing became too great. Compartmentalizing at times can help a person cope with difficult and painful situations. It can be a form of self-protection. I often used this when I was sorting through the difficult phases of

Jason's illness. However, when an individual compartmentalizes too much and misses the big picture of reality, it becomes a problem, not a help.

# Neonatal Intensive Care
# Unit Experience

With Jason's extended stay in the NICU, I now knew the importance of my experience as a NICU nurse. I knew how to deal with all the tubes, IVs, ostomy bag and this and that connected to Jason. I had only worked in a neonatal intensive care unit as a nurse for a year, but this experience was quite valuable. My husband had to learn quickly about Jason's medical condition, but he learned well. He was a real trooper. He was out of his comfort zone for sure, but he learned how to hold Jason with all the wires, ileostomy bag and IVs on Jason's little body. I have always said we make a good pair of bookends because we have very opposite strengths and skill sets to deal with life. Fortunately, our boys received a nice blend of us both.

I could not feed Jason until his ileostomy bag was removed and his small intestines were reconnected. Up to that point, he was receiving all his nourishment from hyperalimentation (liquid nutrition through an IV). It was a challenge for the neonatologist to sustain Jason this way for such a long time. Maintaining weight and balancing his electrolytes were significant feats to achieve. Somehow the neonatologist managed this adequately until the surgeon successfully reconnected Jason at the eight-week mark.

When I would come to visit Jason, I had a system. I would move a standing set of upright curtains from somewhere in the unit and place them around us very tightly. I would also confiscate a rocking chair from somewhere in the unit. This way, Jason and I could have some private time together. I tried to block out, as much as possible, the scene of other sick children and sounds of alarms going off around us. I would ever so gingerly pick Jason up and rock and sing to him for a few hours at each of my visits. I would stroke his beautiful hair, kiss him where there wasn't a tube or bag and think of us being home.

I found out that when Jason would be able to eat, he would not be able to have breast milk. He would have to take special CF formula with CF digestive enzymes. I learned this after I pumped for several weeks and froze breast milk. Well, now I could return that breast pump to the rental company. Yes, and my husband was very glad he didn't have to hear that breast pump machine again.

Holding, singing and stroking Jason's hair was something that helped him feel comforted from the many sticks, pokes and prodding by medical professionals. I hated it for him, but this was all I could do since I could not feed him. His little face and head full of hair was just beautiful! I focused a lot on this part of his body since it was the only part unscathed. This was critical mother baby bonding time for us. As Jason grew older, we came up with a variety of diversional activities to take his mind off medical procedures while he was hospitalized.

I quickly had to go back to work. I had used up ten weeks of my accrued sick leave while I was on bedrest before Jason's birth. I worked as a psychologist at another hospital right across the street from the hospital where both boys were born and where their neonatal intensive care unit was. My husband and I developed a system that worked well for us. I would get to the hospital for work by seven thirty after I would feed Baker his breakfast and pack his daycare bag. Chase would take him to day care at the church. I would get to my office by seven thirty and would work until about eleven fifty a.m. I would then walk across the street to be with Jason from twelve o'clock until about four. Then I would go back to the hospital to make final rounds and then pick up Baker from day care on the way home. Chase would stop by after work to have some time with Jason. After I got Baker to bed, I would often go back to the hospital to spend a little more time with Jason.

I remember back to my early days as a single young nurse noticing that some pediatric children during the day were not attended by their parents. I found this very unusual at that time. But now it makes perfect sense to me. Some parents had to go back to work to keep insurance, have other kids at home to care for, or simply need to work to pay for medical bills incurred by their child.

I will never forget the day the neonatologist shaved off half of Jason's head of hair. Boy, did this really tick me off. I remember how much that bothered me. The nerve of that doctor. He made my kid look weird in my eyes. There is some exaggeration on my part here just to be truthful. There is a thing called the fierceness of mother love. At that very moment I believed I tapped into that fierceness quite vigorously. Mothers, I know you know what I am talking about. When you think someone has wronged your child an attack mode instinct threatens to surface.

One thing Jason loved, when I would rock, sing and hold him, was to stroke his beautiful head of hair. I loved it too. I was mad, darn it. Why did that doctor have to take that away? I very directly let the neonatologist know of my frustration. I had not been warned ahead of time. I considered this to be an unnecessary altering of Jason's appearance. His head was the only place on his body untouched by IVs and various other medical devices. The neonatologist at that moment was a target for some of my emotions of anger about what was happening to Jason. Yes, parents those feelings of anger and loss of control over what is happening to your child can pop up at any time. Your spouse, or a close family member can be a great resource in times like these. But on this occasion in the neonatal intensive care unit, it was just me and the chief neonatologist in a face-off. Boy was it a face-off! I later apologized for my behavior. As I look back on this event, the nurses in the NICU seemed to get a real kick out of watching this little five-foot-tall woman fussing at the chief neonatologist in the unit. Anyway, I did apologize to this doctor. But still, he could have warned me.

I don't know how I would have made it through the difficult times when the boys were in the NICU without the support of my girlfriends, church friends, family, and an especially close Sunday-school teacher. I remember one day when my Sunday school teacher, who was also a minister, came to visit me and Jason in the NICU. It was a bad day for Jason. I blurted out to my Sunday school teacher that I didn't understand why Jason had to go through all this suffering. I said that he had done no wrong and he is just a baby. My Sunday school teacher wisely smiled at me and said that God is big enough to handle my anger? He went on to say that God was not going to leave me even if I did get angry at him. These were profound words coming from someone I respected. I felt calmer after he told me that. Social support was huge for me during so many of the difficult days when the boys were in the NICU. Parents, I encourage you to tap into your support resources when you feel overwhelmed with what is going on with you and your child.

# Jason's Intestinal Reconnection and Feeding

Finally, eight weeks passed, and the surgeon did Jason's intestinal reconnection. At last, Jason got rid of the ileostomy bag and was able to eat from a bottle. What a joy it was to give him nourishment from a bottle. Jason had to take pancreatic digestive enzymes in applesauce before he could take a bottle with CF formula. I had to learn to put a very tiny spoon full of applesauce in a medicine cup and pour some pancreatic enzymes from a capsule into the cup. I had to manage to get this in his tiny mouth and get him to swallow it. This was not an easy task for sure. Jason had to learn early to eat a little applesauce in order to get his enzymes. Enzymes help CF individuals absorb needed nutrition, especially the fats. After Jason was old enough to swallow enzyme capsules, we stopped the applesauce. To this day, Jason hates applesauce and never eats it. I certainly don't blame him for that.

One day I was late going to see Jason in the NICU at my regular twelve o'clock arrival time. I didn't get there until just after twelve thirty. I think Jason had been in the unit about seven weeks by then. Well, on that day, the chief neonatologist met me at the door of the NICU as I was scrubbing in to go into the unit. He seemed frustrated and irritated with me. At the same time, I heard a seemingly familiar voice screaming a blood curdling scream at the top of his lungs. Was that my kid? The neonatologist told me to never be late coming to see Jason again. He said that beginning around twelve o'clock Jason had started crying uncontrollably and could not be comforted by the nurses. He also told me it had upset all the other babies in the unit. I knew as a psychologist that children can be quickly conditioned to the comfort of a mother's touch and voice. I witnessed this firsthand with my own child. As soon as I got to Jason's bedside and started talking to him and touching him, he quickly quieted down. I had no idea that Jason could cry so loudly. Sometimes, as parents, we think, is that really my child acting a certain way or demonstrating that questionable behavior? Oh, it must have come from the other side of the family. He didn't get it from me. Well, so you say. To this day I still remember that scene in the NICU.

Because of the extended time Jason was in the hospital, I was less visible for Baker. This was hard for Baker to understand. All Baker knew was that his preschool schedule had changed, and something was different. He was having a lot of family and parent friends taking him different places. Baker demonstrated a noticeable amount of separation anxiety during these several weeks. He had some loud and long crying spells when I would leave the house or drop him off at preschool. During this time, he learned to suck his thumb and had a very close relationship with "Special Bear" (his favorite stuffed animal). He wouldn't go anywhere without Special Bear. We also learned that Baker could throw a temper tantrum when things didn't go his way. Yes, those terrible twos were quite visible during our current family situation. No one would have suspected that this very loud and vocal child had had a lung problem at birth.

# Jason Gets to Come Home

Finally, Jason was well enough to come home after ten weeks in the NICU. Did I have everything ready for the trip home? I thought so. Am I prepared for the journey? I prayed so. I remember the surgeon telling me, "How well Jason will do will directly depend on your care." What a heavy statement to make to a mother of a young child with CF. I thought to myself, how can he know that? For darn sure I was going to give Jason the best care I could possibly give him. There is some truth to the belief that conscientious care affects a child's overall prognosis with so many different types of illnesses. However, CF can vary so much from one child to another and take a course all its on. Some CF kids have a real tough go in life no matter how diligent the parents may be. Then there are other CF kids who have a much easier life. I still question the absoluteness of the surgeon's final parting statement to me. I really wished I had not heard this. But I did hear this and often felt overly responsible when Jason would get sick. I would ask myself if there was something I did or didn't do that contributed to the exacerbation of his illness. I had to do some "self-talk" to get my mind straight on this. Parents you also may have to watch for this in raising your child with a chronic health condition. Sometimes a child's illness will take a course of its own no matter how diligently parents care for that child.

When Jason, Chase and I came home we were greeted by Jason's grandmother, his older brother and a beautiful arrangement of balloons which had been sent by Dr. Sue, the OB/GYN who delivered Jason. She kept up with his due date for discharge. She was a great support to me with Jason's illness.

Initially, Jason only had digestive problems related to his CF. We religiously followed the enzyme routine before giving formula or, as he grew, introducing solid foods. There were no daily respiratory treatments directed by his CF pulmonary doctor when we were discharged from the hospital. Jason, at that time, did not have any pulmonary component to his CF and no lung treatments were recommended. However, about nine months later his respiratory problems surfaced. Fortunately, my mother, who was a nurse, was keeping him that day. She called me at work to tell me about Jason's breathing difficulty. I quickly came home and immediately took him to the ER. After that ER visit, we began giving breathing treatments routinely twice a day and more often if he was sick. We gave him chest percussion therapy (CPT) which was a clapping of the cupped hands on the back and chest to help loosen secretions in his lungs. Jason grew and we continued Jason's breathing treatments. Various new drugs became available and were prescribed to help liquify the mucous in his lungs. Jason received some form of breathing treatments and CPT at least twice a day until he received a double lung transplant at age twenty-five.

For the first few months after Jason came home from the hospital my mother came to the house and kept Jason while I worked. She was an RN and had been an OB nurse for many years. I did not worry about Jason when she was keeping him. She was a natural with handling babies. I am not sure how I would have managed going back to work right off the bat with a CF infant at home. This was a big relief for both Chase and me as we learned how to balance our lives with a child with CF and another two-year-old child too. My mother's reassurance that Jason looked and acted like any other baby always made me feel good.

After four months, it was time to get a nanny for the in-home care Jason needed. I will never forget my two young nannies, Linda and Tara, who took care of the boys while I worked. I worked four ten-hour days a week. I kept the fifth day free to be able to go to the school each boy attended and have scheduled routine doctor visits. The school activities for each boy were very important to me. I wanted Baker and Jason to have parental representation at school. I know this is not always possible for working parents and I was glad it could work for me. Balancing work and being involved with the different activities of your child can be a real challenge at times. I remember how helpful it was when the nanny learned how to cook a few meals for us for dinner. We all greatly appreciated any effort in this department.

# Trying to Live Like a Normal Family

As a psychologist, I have seen people with medical illness also experience psychological issues circling around dependence/independence and loss of autonomy. I was going to try my best not to let this be the case with Jason and Baker. So in psychological terms, my husband and I mainstreamed and normalized things as much as possible for both boys. Let's take sports as an example. Swimming was our first recreational sporting activity. We did the typical mother baby swim class at the local YMCA with each boy. They both loved the water as much as Chase and I did. These classes were very enjoyable for us.

There was one event around the mother baby swim class with Baker that I remember vividly to this day. One day, I took Baker with me to my mother-in-law's house to swim when he was nine months old. I told Mom Rogers about the mother-baby swim class. I got in her pool with Baker to show her how he could swim under water like he had done with the teacher in swim class two days before. The teacher had instructed me on how to do this and assured me it would work out great. Folks, this did not play out like I had intended. In fact, it was a disaster! I thought I almost drowned my child. My mother-in-law watched as I submerged Baker in the water to swim to her. He quickly surfaced gulping water and needing air. Needless to say, I never tried that again with either boy. Baker did grow up to be an excellent swimmer and was on the swim team in high school. Jason was also a very good swimmer although he chose not to be on a swim team. We learned from Jason's CF doctor that swimming was a very good sport for people with CF. It was believed that the exercise, and chlorinated water that helped to fight bacteria, seemed to help cut down with some lung infections. This is what we were told by the

CF doctors and it made good sense to us. We spent a good deal of the boys' early years around the pool swimming.

At three years of age both boys started soccer. Soccer was the first organized sport both boys entered. We had fun memories of those very early years in sports. I chuckle to myself when I recall the very first soccer game Baker played in. He scored a beautiful goal. He was so proud of himself. He looked over at me and Chase with a big smile. He knew the ball was supposed to go in the goal. We had practiced this at home many times. Unfortunately, the goal was for the opposing team. I took note of this and on the way home purchased an additional goal for practice.

Both boys excelled in sports until Jason's lungs started to decline and Baker got ulcerative colitis and had a colectomy at age ten. From age ten to twelve sports was on the backburner for Baker. For Jason, the running usually helped his lungs. I had heard from Jason's medical team that the more he could use his lungs aerobically through exercise the better it was for his lung function. Exercise helped Jason to expand his lungs and get rid of unwanted mucous which blocked air passages. From ages three to twelve years of age Jason was very fast and good in soccer. Other parents often commented about how fast and quick Jason was. He was "low to the ground" but quite the competitor for a good while on the soccer field. I remember in one game he scored two goals, but his team still lost. As we walked off the field, we were shocked to hear him say "my team sucks." We wondered where this comment came from, but Jason went on to say that all his teammates said it. Chase and I quietly chuckled a little but quickly corrected him. Jason played soccer every spring until he was in the ninth grade and could not run much anymore. He then became the soccer manager for his high school team, and he stopped playing all organized sports because of his advancing CF disease.

Baker on the other hand, after recovering from his colectomy, continued to play soccer on traveling teams throughout most of his high school years. He also played on the high school varsity team. He was an awesome midfielder and knew how to muscle himself around in this sport. He was quick and strong and understood the game of soccer very well.

We started baseball with T-ball at age four. I say we, because any parent of a child playing baseball knows how many practices and games are required each week. I had two playing baseball most of the time. It was always rushed trying to get Jason's breathing treatments in before the multiple game schedule we kept. Both boys played baseball until we came to the kid's pitch level. When we hit kid's pitch baseball was not for Jason anymore. Jason was not going to let another kid throw a fast ball at him. It was challenging that year to get Jason to stand even somewhat near the batter's box to receive a pitch. That was the last year of baseball for Jason. Baker continued with baseball and did well. He became the designated catcher for his team.

In middle school Jason ran cross country for two years. I was a little hesitant about this due to the asthma component he developed during this time as part of his CF. He insisted that he wanted to be with his friends who were going to do cross country. I agreed, but it was harder than I thought for me to watch him push himself and at times struggle to breathe. He was usually near the last to cross the finish line. However, he had some real encouraging teammates and supportive coaches who always cheered him on. At this time, I encouraged Jason to try tennis. This was a better sport for him. It let him run and exert himself at his own pace. His competitive nature was still evident, as he always hated to lose.

My husband and I even agreed for Jason to play basketball. He had good eye hand coordination and was a good shot. He was just very short for this sport. He loved basketball and did this for five years He was not one who was able to get a lot of rebounds in a game, but he had a lot of fun. Chase and I did the typical thing for both boys, taking turns as team dad and team mom. These were fun years for us all, but very busy years too.

Baker was a very good athlete in all sports. He was unusually good in soccer, baseball, wrestling, water skiing, and track until he developed ulcerative colitis at age ten. He had a couple of years of just okay performance in sports until he recovered from his illness. Maybe a more appropriate way to describe his recovery is that he learned to adapt to the problems that go along with not having a colon. During the eighth-grade year, in wrestling, he was undefeated in his weight class. I will never forget what the mom sitting next to me said at one of Baker's wrestling matches, "now Baker is really back."

With sporting events, we were always conscious to pay attention to each boys' nutritional needs with good food, frequent snacks, plenty of fluids and regular enzymes for Jason. We packed in extra calories for both boys during games and frequent practices. Jason sweated like crazy on exercise which a lot of CF kids do. We were conscious to provide Gatorade religiously for him and to be liberal with salt on his food during the summer seasons. Baker also needed close attention to make sure he stayed well hydrated because of his increased bowel activity and fluid loss from this. CF kids lose more sodium in their sweat production than non-CF kids. Electrolyte depletion, primarily sodium, was always something to watch for with Jason. Jason never was much of a junk eater as a child which was a good thing. I can't say the same about Baker. Baker always had a sweet tooth. Even to this day Jason, makes good food choices. He learned early the importance of good nutrition because he desperately wanted to get taller and stronger. Fortunately, now, Baker is a very healthy eater and watches his diet closely.

As parents, we believed in having Jason and Baker participate in as many activities as possible like other kids their own age until their illnesses limited them. We were protective, but focused on as much normal growth, development, and mainstreaming as possible. This is what worked for us. When participation in sports was not going to be a positive experience, we switched to other activities that were less physical.

# Jason Asserts Some Independence with His Health Care

I remember the year when Jason was especially persistent with his request to spend the night at a friend's house. Up to that point, his friends always came to our house because of Jason's breathing treatments. Well, at age six, we taught Jason how to calculate his breathing medicine in a dropper. He had to learn how to add medicine to the aerosol chamber of his breathing machine. We let Jason control his own medication administration for his night away from home. I know this may have seemed a little risky, but this fostered more independence and greater participation by Jason in his own health care. Did I worry about Jason's night away from home? Absolutely, I worried, but we gave it a try. This first spend the night away actually worked out just fine. Parents when you feel ready, and it is feasible, I encourage you to try giving more ownership to your child for his or her health care. This can do a lot to foster independence in a child with health problems. I think this can also help encourage more natural age appropriate experiences.

Over time, new CPT devices came out that the CF child could do on their own. Jason used the flutter or acapella when he would spend the night away from home. These were hand-held devices to help clear his air passages by vibration when he would inhale and exhale into the device. Later the chest vest was invented as another option for CPT after breathing treatments. The chest vest was also something that Jason could manage himself as he got a little older. This, too, gave him more control over his needed treatments.

As Jason got older, it became more of an effort each morning to get all of Jason's breathing treatments in before school. Additional medications were added to his treatments taking thirty minutes to complete. After that, Jason needed a good fifteen to thirty minutes of CPT. Try doing sixty minutes of breathing treatments twice a day with an active, young growing boy. This was quite a challenge, especially during teenage years. When he was sick, we were instructed to do four treatments a day. This was hard to do. No, really, it was quite rough. It felt like so much of Jason's day was tied to his aerosol machine. He became very resentful of this. I certainly understood why, too. This often kept him from doing other activities with his friends or just things he wanted to do. Along with watching TV and playing computer games during this time, he would read and write. To this day, Jason is a very good reader and writer. This time was useful for some of his less active areas of personal interest.

# Baker Gave Us a Scare

Baker gave us a scare when he was five years old. He was in kindergarten at the time. Baker developed an unusual problem going to the bathroom, and he started losing weight. This was right around the time he was collecting tin can tabs for a school project. This was when we thought he must have picked up the bug. Baker began having diarrhea and greasy, fatty, smelly stools just like the CF kids do without proper pancreatic enzymes to absorb essential nutrients like fats.

I thought, okay, what is going on with Baker? I knew the earlier sweat test was negative. Could this have been wrong? I took Baker to Jason's CF/GI doctor. She did a stool sample on Baker to test for fat malabsorption. The test came back positive for fat malabsorption. This doctor told me Baker would need genetic testing to confirm her suspicion that Baker did in fact have CF. I was very concerned about this. No, I kind of freaked out about this!

This just did not feel right. I went to my wise pediatrician for another opinion. He suggested I go back to this CF/GI doctor and ask for the most probable cause of Baker's problem. He suggested I ask for a stool culture for amoeba and parasite. I did what he suggested. Thankfully, it was only a parasite Baker had picked up that caused the fat malabsorption syndrome. He was treated for parasites and quickly returned to normal in about two weeks. Having the CF possibility for Baker resurface again was quite frightening. After that, I never felt confident about this CF specialist.

# When It Is Time for a
# Second Opinion

A month or so later I took Jason to his regular pediatrician for his yearly checkup. My pediatrician was curious to know how often Jason was seeing the CF/GI specialist. He was focused on Jason's abdomen as he continued to mash here and there around Jason's stomach and abdominal area. I told him that Jason was being seen every three months. He said that he felt an enlarged liver on Jason. He quizzed me if anyone had mentioned this to me. I shook my head with a "no." Then, I quickly got by Jason's side, palpated his liver area and felt an enlarged liver. I felt my hand go a little numb.

The next day, I scheduled an appointment with the CF/GI specialist. I brought Jason's liver issue up to her. She somewhat dismissed my concern about Jason's liver. She indicated it was a fatty liver that CF kids often develop. She went over some recent labs of Jason's and told me not to worry. Well, I did worry. Things just didn't feel right. Parents, especially mothers, who often have a sixth sense when it comes to your child's wellbeing, pay attention to those feelings of unrest. I knew right then and there it was time to switch CF specialists.

About a month later, we saw another CF specialist. I took all of Jason's labs with me. Before he even examined Jason, he said the labs indicated that Jason may be having some liver fibrosis (hardening) and possibly beginning liver cirrhosis. The CF specialist palpated Jason's abdomen, and confirmed what he thought was going on. He also had me palpate the enlarged and rough bordered liver. The CF specialist said only about one out of one hundred kids with CF will have liver disease. We were not beating the odds with this stuff. The doctor suggested a liver biopsy as soon as Jason could be scheduled. He also put Jason on a medicine called Actigall. This medicine was to help slow down the potential liver disease. The liver biopsy showed liver fibrosis with early cirrhosis. I heard my voice quietly whisper, "He is only six."

This CF doctor took great care of Jason for many years. He was what I would call a "Brainiac" with a good bedside manner. He had a bad habit of mumbling, but he was always direct and upfront with me. I could handle that. He told me Jason would probably need a liver transplant before adulthood. For me, I cope better when I have adequately prepared myself with medical information needed to push forward with Jason's evolving health problems. I leaned on my support resources of family and friends. They helped tremendously. Every time I got some bad news, I had two especially close friends I talked to in addition to my two older sisters.

# My Greatest Fear: Something Is Wrong with My Other Child!

Baker was sick. I quit work for almost two years when Baker was ten years old. At that time in Baker's life he was the fastest kid in his grade, and I think for the elementary school. He was excellent at soccer, baseball, gymnastics, swimming, and skiing. He was muscular, strong, and fast at most any sport he played. But something happened to him that fourth grade year that was life changing! He picked up a virus at school like some of his close friends did, but his virus didn't go away. He tried to go back to school. However, he kept having off and on GI symptoms of nausea, vomiting, and diarrhea. I took him to the doctor several times. The third time we went to the pediatrician, he sent us to a pediatric GI doctor. The GI specialist did a colonoscopy and found an ulcerated area in Baker's colon. He prescribed prednisone, and antibiotics for the ulcerated area. However, this did not help. Baker began having blood in his stool and continued to experience nausea, vomiting and abdominal cramping. He started losing a good bit of weight. I became very worried and could not watch my son go downhill anymore. As a parent, not just because I had a nursing background, I knew something was seriously wrong with my child. He was so sick and frightened. He kept a lot of this fear inside. At ten years old, he had no idea why his body was failing him. There was no question, his body was seriously failing him.

It seemed that the doctors did not have the answers to what was wrong with Baker or the specific treatment to correct his problem. The steroids and antibiotics had not been helpful. My mother's protective instincts were escalating at this time. Finally, an aggressive move was made to put him in the hospital. He was admitted to the children's hospital and stayed there for a full six weeks.

After Baker was admitted to the hospital, he was not allowed to take anything by mouth for five full weeks to rest and hopefully heal his colon. All his nutrition was by hyperalimentation (nutrition through an IV tube). I remember how hard it was for me to watch Baker hallucinate about food. He imagined he saw types of food in the air around his bed. Baker begged me for something to eat. Along with being severely hungry, I am sure the IV steroids he was put on contributed to the hallucinations. I was a strong advocate for Baker and asked the doctors if they could at least try some clear liquids. Clear liquids were tried, but this irritated his colon and increased bleeding. Over time the desire for food went away as he became sicker. The virus he picked up apparently had ulcerated his entire colon. He lost twenty pounds in about five weeks.

The morning starting the sixth week, a change in direction of treatment was made for Baker. The surgeon came in and said, "We are going to have to remove Baker's colon, now." The surgeon indicated that there was no other option to pursue at that point in time. There was a lot of conversation between me, my husband and the surgeon. The surgeon was clear with us about what to expect regarding subsequent surgeries needed for Baker. The surgeon indicated that Baker would have an ostomy bag for a few months and then other surgery would be performed on his intestines. I remember the night before his colectomy. I got beside Baker's hospital bed at night on my knees and prayed.

The ulcerated colon was taken out and an ostomy bag was attached to Baker's side. Then, Baker could eat again. He started gaining weight as soon as food was reintroduced. The morning after his colectomy he looked so much better. Through my work as a nurse, I had often seen that when a diseased part gets removed from a patient's body how dramatically they can start improving with proper medical treatment. Baker's color looked pinker and brighter, and he seemed more comfortable. One of the first things he wanted to eat was a po-boy sandwich from his favorite sandwich shop. It didn't matter to us that it was breakfast time. We were going to give him whatever he wanted to eat. His grandmother bought one and brought it to the hospital. He ate every bite of that sandwich. We were so happy to see Baker get to eat and enjoy the simple pleasure of food. After Baker began eating, he continued to improve and started to get some of his physical strength back.

We had to adapt to Baker having an ostomy bag on his side. My husband and I were well trained on how to care for an ostomy bag before we ever left the hospital. One week after the colectomy, Baker came home. We gave Baker's ostomy a name. This way, Baker and I could talk about the condition of his ostomy bag in public without alerting others. I suggested two or three names, and Baker chose "Burt." We had many conversations about Burt in all sorts of places and no one ever knew what we were referencing.

Burt was a lifesaver. Had Baker's colon not been removed he would have probably continued to bleed out and lose weight. The surgery was something that had to happen. There was some question among the doctors whether Baker had crohn's disease or ulcerative colitis. The surgeon stated it looked very much like ulcerative colitis when he removed the colon. When the pathology report was completed, it confirmed that Baker had ulcerative colitis.

# Baker Gets Discharged One
# Week after Surgery

Baker got out of the hospital right around the end of the school year. We had not planned our beach vacation yet. Baker was worried about how Burt would tolerate swimming. So as most any mother would do, I improvised for a swimsuit. I bought Baker a short wetsuit so he could keep his ostomy bag covered as he enjoyed the water. We kept our newfound friend Burt as a private matter. We learned that friends did not quite know how to deal with Baker's ostomy. He had a couple of quasi friends who saw it early on and their comments to him made him very self-conscious about it. After that, he only let a very close couple of friends see it.

Life was good. Baker gained fifteen pounds back of the twenty that he had lost. Up to this point, we thought this was the hardest thing Baker would have to go through. Now, it was time for Baker to let Burt go and have the surgical reconnection. We had no idea how hard this was going to be. We had no idea!

Parents, when your children are young, they depend on you to be their strongest advocates. They depend on you to make the best decisions you can possibly make about their health care through your own research of the illness and your communication with their doctors. As the children age, they hopefully will gradually move toward taking steps towards ownership of their own illness and begin to make some independent decisions. The next decision Chase and I had to make for Baker was very tough. It required a lot of personal medical research, and medical information and guidance from his doctors. This decision related to the removal of Baker's ostomy bag and either a J pouch procedure or ileal pull though procedure. We chose the ileal pull-through. This was a direct attachment of Baker's small intestine to an extremely small amount of rectal tissue.

With a wonderfully skilled surgeon, an ileo-pull through was successfully performed. This meant the ileum of the small intestine was connected directly to about one to two centimeters of rectal tissue. Over time, the goal of this surgery was to have the small intestine adapt in size to the large intestine and take over most of its functions. According to the surgeon, we went the harder route initially but with less potential problems in the long run. Also, the surgeon told us this surgical technique would require one less surgery for Baker. The surgeon told us that J pouch individuals more often had something called "pouchitis" and infections more than the ileal pull-through surgery. To this day, Baker has never had "pouchitis." We did extensive research and leaned heavily on our skilled surgeon's knowledge base. I do not know what surgical recommendations are most often made as treatment options for ulcerative colitis currently. My husband and I made the best decision we could at that time given the information we had. Hopefully, we made the right one. Parents, I know at times you may also be faced with very tough medical decisions about your child's care. Weighing the pros and cons of different treatment options can be most challenging.

Baker had no idea he would have a few months of bowel incontinence after the ileal pull through. He was prescribed two medicines, Lomotil and Imodium, after surgery to help to slow down gastrointestinal motility. Additionally, I did some behavior modification and shaping behavior with Baker. I did this during the day and night to help Baker pick up on early signals that he needed to go to the bathroom. He lost weight again due to the surgery and profound stress to his body. The goal of this surgery, as I understand it, was that over time the small intestine would enlarge and take over most of the work that the large intestine did. But this took a good full year and even longer. Not having a colon most certainly still presents challenges for Baker.

Does a person's illness influence personality or does the personality cause and significantly impact the illness? This is a question I have often heard asked. I am not sure there is an exact answer to that question. However, I did watch Baker become withdrawn and depressed. He lost self-confidence in himself for about a two-year period. He missed Burt and the predictability of Burt's elimination function. Up to this point, this was the hardest year for me emotionally in dealing with either boys' health problems.

The emotional aspect of this adjustment was quite difficult for Baker. I used every bit of psychology I knew to help him cope with this life changing event. After a year and a half or so Baker gained enough weight and strength to reengage in sports. It really took two years to bounce back with his full strength.

He went on to play baseball, wrestle, exceed at cross country and become a very good mid-field soccer player. However, it took time to bounce back. It was harder and longer than we expected. Three or four years after Baker's surgery I was asked to be a speaker for the annual crohn's and colitis nurse's convention. I had a lot to say about what Baker and I had learned and how he adapted. We used some basic behavioral conditioning techniques that were beneficial and a lot of open communication. The support and acceptance by the parents and other family members are crucial for a more positive adjustment to a body image change like what Baker had to experience.

# The Importance of Support
# for the Primary Caregiver

I was going to throw up If I heard one more time that God doesn't give you more than what you can handle. Or better yet, with all your training God knew what He was doing when He gave you Jason and Baker. Sometimes I think people just don't know what to say when a person is really going through difficulties in life. I think this awkwardness happens because people really don't completely think through what they are saying. Another thought I have is that individuals, when talking to a parent of a sick child, may not think things through from that parents' perspective. It could be the timing of what was said as opposed to what was actually spoken. It is really okay to just be quiet. Just be present and/or give a heartfelt embrace. In my training I learned about a prominent psychological theorist by the name of Carl Rogers. He was very successful with his approach to therapy. He believed in giving individuals positive regard, attentively listening to them and reflecting on their comments. He developed client centered therapy. In my training I have learned that when an individual believes they are being listened to attentively, it can start changing brain chemistry of that individual in a positive way. Don't forget that it is okay at times just to listen to people when they are hurting.

I want to point out that there certainly may be times, during your health care journey with your child, when expression of feelings of anger to someone you feel close to is needed. It was for me anyway. At a certain point in the boys' illnesses, I checked in with a psychiatrist to more fully express a range of emotions. I will never forget the psychiatrist who helped me during some difficult times with the boys' illnesses. She was just what I needed. I learned over time that she had lost a child to an unusual illness. She understood my greatest fear. The fear being, that I could lose one or possibly both of my children. I don't believe this was an accidental referral from my OB/GYN for therapy. I saw her off and on for a few years just to check in when my boys were having extreme health challenges. A professionally trained person, to help individuals cope in times of crisis, can be most beneficial. For a change, I was on the receiving end of counseling and not the deliverer.

I have witnessed pent up emotions such as anger, grief, and despair lead to other psychological symptoms such as depression. If left unchecked, intense negative emotions and pessimism can take a toll on the body both physically and psychologically. The parent's emotional needs, as the care giver of a sick child, should receive attention. I know on a personal level, when the care giver gets physically exhausted it can take a toll on one's emotions. When our bodies get *physically exhausted, our* emotions may not be as resilient. I believe when we worry too much about what might happen to us in life, we can often miss out on some of life's true joys. For me, during some difficult times with both my boys' illnesses, I claimed the scripture Jeremiah 29:11 that says, God has a plan for each of our lives. I knew God had a plan for Jason and Baker. I just had to figure out how to tap into that plan.

# More Discouraging News

One Saturday morning, before a playoff soccer game, Jason came downstairs to the kitchen while I was cooking pancakes for breakfast. I told him he needed to get dressed in home colors for the game. I also stated he needed to do his breathing treatment before breakfast. Jason was eleven at the time. I will never forget what he told me. He looked at me somewhat anxiously and said that there was something wrong with one of his balls. Jason said, "my ball is getting bigger." Mind you now, my mind was on the pancakes and sausage I was cooking. I responded with something like that happens when you grow older. Jason said, "No, Mom, it is really big." "Something is wrong with one of them." Well, Jason's scrotum was the size of half a tennis ball! I called the pediatrician's office, told them my concerns, and got an appointment for the afternoon. There was no pain or redness in the area Jason was pointing to. Jason reminded me that this was a final play-off game and he was an important forward on his team. He was adamant that he could not miss this important game. So like any good mother knows to do, I became creative and grabbed one of my husband's socks. We wrapped his scrotum up with the sock. We made sure it was padded and protected very well. I instructed Jason that during the game, he could do no heroics or slide tackles of any sort. I told him that if the slightest discomfort started, he would have to come off the field. Jason promised he would be extra careful. This got us through the game. Oh, and by the way, Jason did score a goal.

A couple of hours later we were at the pediatrician's office. He told us that Jason had an inguinal hernia. We followed up with a pediatric surgeon the next week and had his surgery without any problems. We received confirmation on some disappointing news, though. The surgeon confirmed that Jason could not biologically have children. Jason had no vas deferens (the tube that allows sperm to travel to the opening of the head of the penis). I knew CF boys most commonly could not father children. I was told by Jason's surgeon that this is a common occurrence with male children with CF. Having this confirmed by the surgeon was another loss.

# I Gave My Testimony at Church

After some time went by, I felt the need to give my testimony at church. We had such strong prayer warriors at the church where we attended at that time. They brought us meals, they visited me when I was on bedrest, they prayed with us. They cut our grass at different times while we were at the hospital. Several men even came to our house and helped my husband Chase finish the storage shed he had started building before Jason was born. Trauma and difficulties in life, I believe, can bring someone closer to God or push them further away. For me, the difficulties brought me closer and I leaned on God for extra strength. I was equipped with professional knowledge to help me cope with difficulties, but I needed God's comfort and guidance, especially during this time. I have always done a lot of public speaking and presentations in my professional life. But on this occasion, I spoke strictly from the heart. I spoke to my church family thanking them and sharing what I had learned through Jason's and Baker's medical problems. For me, this was the most emotional speech I had ever given. I believe that fellow Christians serve as the arms and hands of God on this earth. My family benefited from other Christians reaching their arms out to us during these difficult times.

# Jason Goes to CF Camp

I think it is often helpful for people with physical illness to have a positive connection with other people who are dealing with similar difficulties. We all have a need for connectedness to others, especially when there are some similarities of sorts. Again, I say a positive connection. It is helpful for an individual to see other people with their diagnosis coping successfully with their challenges. I remember how often I would meet older CF kids at the CF clinic who looked like they were doing fairly well with their illness. This was encouraging to me and Jason. We would ask them what treatments they found to be most helpful, as well as what they did about diet and exercise. Some of the older young adult patients would emphasize to Jason the importance of taking care of himself and keeping up with his breathing treatments. Having this information come from other CF individuals was a great support to me as the primary care giver.

However, one time connecting with other kids with CF backfired a little. There was a big push by the CF medical team for Jason to go to CF camp. I had resisted this for several years, because up to that point, Jason had been doing well mainstreaming with other kids his age. It sounded like a wonderful experience for kids with CF. When Jason went to camp at age ten, he had never stayed in the hospital overnight for CF treatments. He was fortunate that, even with all the aerosol treatments and enzyme therapy, he had been able to keep up pretty well with his school and church friends.

With the CF clinics' encouragement, we packed up all the necessary items for Jason and off he went to CF camp. All the boys in Jason's cabin at CF camp also had some level of CF and were about Jason's age, give or take a year or two. The CF clinic folks said the experience would be good for Jason and give me a break from his treatments and overall care. My husband and I were looking forward to some date nights that week.

The experience did not go well for Jason. What happened was that this experience scared him. He came home fearful that he was going to die soon. He said a lot of the people at camp talked about the CF kids who had recently died. Jason thought he was going to be next. There were some positive things that came from this, though. This did give us an opportunity to talk about how well he was doing and the new treatments coming out. I showed him newspaper articles about the discovery of the CF gene. It was discovered the summer before he was born. I do want to emphasize that we knew many CF kids who went to camp and had a wonderful experience. It was a great opportunity offered by CF health professionals.

About a week after he returned home, we got back to our normal day to day activities. However, the next summer Jason went to a regular camp. Jason promised me he would do his treatments as supervised by the camp counselor. He came home from the next camp experience a little congested but proud of his accomplishments. This was the route we took for two more summer camps. Then summer camps were no longer possible as Jason's CF disease advanced.

# Fighting for Growth Hormones and Peer Acceptance

The CF checkups were often discouraging. Sometimes, me, myself, and I had to have some bathroom mirror talks to stay in the present. You know those heart to heart talks with yourself to pump yourself up for tough times. Each three-month CF visit was somewhat stressful. Holding our own with health issues was a major victory. However, over time, each CF visit became more discouraging. Jason started having more lung involvement. He wasn't growing properly. I remember numerous times Jason jumped into the car after school complaining about being the smallest person in his grade. He even elaborated on having smaller feet than any of the girls in his grade. Jason said that he was tired of being kidded about being so little. After many times of hearing this, and doing CF research, I realized that CF kids often are more deficient in growth hormones. The next day, Jason got in the car after school and gave me a similar greeting. Later that month, I scheduled an endocrinology appointment to address Jason's small stature. Unfortunately, the first endocrinologist seemed to minimize our situation and told us just to focus on good nutrition and extra calories. I had obsessively payed attention to this all twelve years of Jason's life. This warranted a second endocrinologist's opinion. The second endocrinologist did a growth hormone test on Jason. The test showed that Jason was indeed deficient. Jason was put on growth hormone injections and he started growing like a weed. I was told by Jason's CF specialist that it is important for the CF child to grow adequately in puberty so the lungs can more fully develop as well. To this day, he is a pretty good height for a CF kid, and tall genes are not something that run in our family to start with.

# Coping with Liver Disease

We went through several years of taking medicine to attempt to slow down the liver cirrhosis. I was told by the CF doctor at that time that only about one percent of kids with CF develop liver cirrhosis. Jason's liver, according to the doctor, began laying down scar tissue and decreasing liver function. The congestion in the liver due to scarring and increased pressure caused Jason's abdomen to protrude. His spleen also enlarged. As the spleen enlarged, while Jason was still playing soccer, he had to wear a padded belt around his abdomen to protect his spleen from injury.

I remember the years Jason would come home from school and ask me if he was fat? He wanted to know if it looked like his stomach stuck out. He got around to telling me that his friends at school suggested he go on a diet and probably needed to lose some weight. Like any good parent would do, when Jason needed reassurance about his body image, I gave it to him. Jason's arms and legs were quite skinny, and his stomach did protrude. The liver disease was advancing and began causing a shrinkage in the size of the muscles in his extremities. I remember one night, what Jason said to me after I reassured him that he looked just perfect and handsome to me. He said that he would accept the handsome but reminded me that I had always told him no one is perfect. I stood corrected and thanked my child for his wisdom. I then would state that he looked just fine to me. In my eyes that is what I would let myself see. But at night, as my mind wandered, I would know this was not the true case.

Shopping with Jason to get clothes that looked like his peers was difficult. His liver enlarged along with his spleen making it hard to find clothes that would fit over his abdomen and not accentuate the large belly he was developing. He hated to go buy clothes. His abdominal veins were very prominent also due to the increased pressure in the liver's circulation. Clothes needed to be loose and not constrictive. It is hard enough any way shopping for clothes with any thirteen-year-old boy. They want so much to blend in with their peer group. We had to be creative with picking clothes for him to wear.

# The CF Routine Impacted
# Family Spontaneity

Wherever we were, all of Jason's life, he had to do two aerosols a day for respiratory maintenance and up to four aerosols a day when he was sick. This was a lot of play time to miss for a kid. There was no such thing as spontaneous sleep over at a friend's house. We had to make sure Jason had all of his aerosol equipment and medications with him before he could stay away from home for a night. I know Baker was tired of having to wait for Jason to get his aerosol treatments in before we could go places. I was extremely organized with the time allotment for breathing treatments. However, I lost count of how many times we were almost late getting places because of the treatments and the needed CPT. Baker would often give Jason a verbal prompt of, "Hurry up bro, we need to go." But there was no hurry up that Jason could do. The aerosols required devoted time. The aerosol noise was also distracting to Baker and Jason when the two boys were playing board games or watching TV. We had to make some adjustments for Baker. Baker needed his own TV space to watch by himself. As Jason's CF disease advanced his treatments would often take a full hour to complete. As an infant and young child Jason seemed to be pretty tolerant of these treatments. He occasionally would fall asleep while I did CPT on his back. But as he got older, he for sure did not like having to do aerosol and the CPT. Oh, and forget about ever having a teenager to baby sit from down the street in your neighborhood. Chase and I always had to prepare far in advance for date nights with a mature, confident adult willing to do breathing treatments before Jason's bedtime.

# Normal Childhood Injuries

Jason and Baker had the normal childhood injuries of active boys. Jason broke a wrist playing basketball at camp. He broke two toes playing soccer. Oh yes, he got stitches in his head the time his brother threw a boomerang at him. Baker was a good brother in that he treated Jason like a normal healthy brother as much as he possibly could. Baker broke a bone in his foot playing soccer, had a problem with a growth plate in his leg, and got a few stitches in his head from a swing set injury. I remember when the boys were young, Baker would always win the scuffles. Jason had to learn to be sly and sneaky to get back at his brother. Jason had somewhat of a bad habit of kind of cheating to win at things when he was outsized by his brother. He had quite a competitive spirit. I remember the day Jason hid Baker's first grade bookbag with his homework in it. We never could find the bag that morning as we were rushing off to school and work. Baker had to stay after school a little while for being late and not having his homework. Later that evening Jason showed me where he hid Baker's bag. Boy, was Baker ever mad at his brother for that prank he played on him.

We engaged in as many activities as we could to live as normal a life as possible for Jason and Baker. We did learn a few things the hard way. We stopped snow skiing after the third year due to Jason's limited lung capacity and the elevation in Colorado. Jason and I hung out in the condo most of the week the last time we tried snow skiing. We enjoyed vacations at the lake and beach after that year. Unfortunately, this was a big disappointment to Baker because he loved snow skiing and was very good at it.

# The Years of Going to the Lake for Vacation

We also had some very good family times as the boys were growing up. Years at the lake and the beach were some of the very best times for us. We had our tough times for sure. But when things were at a place where we could have fun, we tried diligently to do that.

I remember around the time Baker had his intestinal surgery my husband had had the idea of going to Lake Burton for a family lake vacation. He had driven by this lake many times on his motorcycle rides and said it looked like a great place to have a vacation. I could not wrap my head around this because Baker and I were in survival mode post operatively. My husband said that whenever we get over all this illness, we need to have something fun to focus on. We disagreed on the timing but boy was this vacation spot a haven for my family. My husband has always been the one to project far ahead on things while I would handle more of the day to day needs of the family. Like I said earlier, my husband and I make a good pair of book ends with our different skill sets.

During our lake vacation years, we made memories that we will never forget. The skiing, tubing, kayaking, swimming, fishing was awesome fun. You would never know we had so much "medical" going on with the kids. We adapted and made the most of all the things we were able to do. Baker wore a wet suit for some of this time, and Jason continued all the breathing treatments he had to do. We played hours of monopoly at night because there was no TV. These were the best years of fun our family had to date.

I don't know who enjoyed the lake house more. We all loved it, but our golden retriever was in dog heaven. She tubed and would knee board with the boys. She would get in the water, dive for rocks on the bottom of the lake and give them to the boys as she surfaced. She was their constant companion in the water and out. The boys would hold onto her tail, and she would pull them through the water. We had two different golden retrievers during the lake vacation years and they both loved it. There was one other important role our golden retriever Brandi served for Baker. As Baker got older and took the boat out by himself, according to Baker and his guy friends, Brandi was an awesome "chick magnet." Oh, and I can't forget the boiled peanuts. There was a country store that made the best boiled peanuts. The boys would kayak down to the store and bring us our daily supply of peanuts and candy to get us through the day. At that point in time, the surroundings of this mountain lake were safe for letting older children venture out a little and feel some independence.

# Summer Beach Trips

We also had some wonderful times at the beach. For several years, when the boys were well enough, my family packed up the typical beach paraphernalia along with all of Jason's aerosol equipment, chest vest and bottles of enzymes and tons of regular medicines. Our car was always jam packed for these trips. We all loved the saltwater, sand and general atmosphere at Saint Augustine beach. There was one summer when Baker required an ostomy bag, that we had to make sure we had an ample supply. Baker's wet suit kept his ostomy bag concealed when he was on the beach and in the water. There were a couple of times, when Baker was body surfing very aggressively, that the seal broke on the ostomy bag and he needed a quick change. Otherwise, for the five months Baker needed and ostomy bag, the wet suit was the perfect trick for all his water sports.

Jason's CF doctors always told us that swimming in a properly chlorinated pool and ocean saltwater was good for CF lung function. The CF doctors told us that the chlorine or salt content of water could help CF kids to fight potential lung infection. I found this to be quite interesting information. So with this advice we made sure Jason had an opportunity to get in plenty of swimming. One thing we did notice though, about the beach and lake, was to be careful about Jason getting too chilled from the wind. It seemed that the beach was always breezy in the evening. Jason would often start to cough at the beach or at the lake if there were too much breezing wind. We made special accommodations for this once we realized this was a problem for him. But sometimes he just got sick no matter what precautions we took. This was just part of having CF. Parents, sometimes getting sick happens no matter how you try to prevent it.

We did everything at the beach that everybody else would do, and maybe even more so. We were a very active family. We swam, road the boogie board, body surfed, fished, flew kites, drove moped bikes, played tennis, shuffleboard, racket ball and putt-putt golf. We made sandcastles and covered each other up with sand. We have some great pictures of the boys diving into the water from off their dad's hands which he held up high over his shoulders. We also took our baseball gloves and baseballs and got in a lot of good practice while we were at the beach. Our boys were fearless warriors, or at least they tried to be with what they had going on physically at the time. There was one family activity that I did not participate in. That activity was eating alligator and turtle at one of the restaurants we always visited. I just couldn't bring myself to do it. But speaking of food, there was an awesome place where we always bought fudge. Fudge was a favorite sweet treat for us all.

# The Love of a Pet

Writing about our golden retriever's fun at the lake made me want to give a special shout out to having a pet. Personally, I had all kinds of pets growing up. One of my favorite pets as a child was my cocker spaniel dog. He was a great companion, and he was especially tolerant of me pulling out my nurse's kit and bandaging different parts of his body with gauze. Sometimes the guy could hardly move if I happened to bandage him too tightly.

Our two golden retrievers were the boys' favorite pets. I remember how our golden retriever, Casey, would climb up the ladder going to the boys play gym in the back yard and take her turn to slide down the slide right after them. We made it even more fun by putting a small kid's pool at the bottom of the slide so she would splash into the water in the pool. This would go on for hours. The boys and Casey would go faster and faster down the slide splashing into the pool water at the bottom. My job was simply to keep the pool filled up with water as they splashed it out.

But at other times the boy's dog, Brandi would stay right by them when they were ill. Our dog Brandi would act like a sphinx. Brandi would be ever so still, keeping watch over her person. She would sense when Jason felt bad or needed company during his aerosol treatments. Brandi knew when Baker became ill and ever so faithfully stood guard by his side to comfort him. Brandi was the sweetest dog I have met to date.

I still on occasion see pets being brought in as therapy at different hospitals and memory care units. For a child, I don't think there is anything quite like the constant companionship of an animal when they feel ill. As the child grows and can take care of the pet's needs, this can also increase the child's sense of independence, responsibility, and enhance self-esteem.

# Jason Develops CF-Related Diabetes

At thirteen years of age Jason presented dramatically with CF related diabetes. I thought shoot! We have another big medical problem to address. My husband said that it seemed like Jason can't get a break. Parents, I know that sometimes right when you think you have everything under control with your child's health needs, something else may pop up unexpectedly. For Jason, he began dropping weight quickly. He started coming in from school, eating and drinking large amounts of food and fluids, and then falling asleep. He was also very irritable which was not like Jason. Yes parents, Jason was more irritable than the average thirteen-year-old teenage boy for sure. If I didn't know my child, I would have sworn that he could have been on drugs. One day after school, he came to the kitchen eating everything he could find and drinking copious amounts of fluids. He acted belligerent and delirious. He then went back to his room and fell asleep. He repeated this cycle another time that evening, and then was hard to awaken. Off to the emergency room we went. When his blood sugar was checked it was six hundred, and he was urinating ketones which suggested diabetes.

He was hospitalized and the doctor started him on insulin injections right away. It was interesting that Jason did not want me giving him his insulin injections. I could help supervise and provide supplies, but he wanted to do the injections himself. While Jason was still in the hospital, we went through a lot of patient teaching about carb counting and calculating insulin for injections. We learned about rotating insulin injection sites and checking blood sugar before meals and at snack time. Jason took ownership of his diabetes regarding his injections. He really kind of demanded it to be honest. He did not want his mother, who was a nurse, being involved in giving him any kind of injection. I respected this, like any good mother would do, and I backed off here. As much as I wanted to get my hands on this, I knew to let Jason handle things because he was thirteen years old. Jason was going to be in charge of his diabetes. He later went on an insulin pump. I had to help him advocate to the doctors to move rather quickly to the insulin pump rather than the injections. The pump fit easier into Jason's lifestyle as a teenager.

Diabetes is often seen in CF individuals. Jason was challenged again to develop resilience in adapting to these ongoing changes in his health.

# Jason Was Baptized

I remember the day Jason was baptized by the youth minister at our church. Jason has always been strong in his walk with the Lord. Family and close friends were there supporting Jason in his affirmation of faith. The youth minister had everyone who was touched by Jason's life to stand up in the congregation. I was amazed at how many lives Jason had already touched at such a young age of thirteen. It was a very moving time as a parent. Both boys were raised in the church, and we have good memories of their years growing up in this environment.

# Jason's Liver Disease Advances

On the way to school one day, I sniffed and asked Jason if he had had time to get a shower last night. Chase and I had just recently talked about Jason's increasing body odor. Along with Jason's abdominal distension, yellowing skin from elevated bilirubin, Jason had increased ammonia levels which caused unpleasant body odor. One of the functions of the liver is to convert ammonia to urea to be excreted by the body. Because of Jason's failing liver, increased ammonia levels and increased bilirubin were present. We had to be creative to find strong body washes, and increased frequency of showering to improve Jason's hygiene. When the liver loses function in cirrhosis, bilirubin levels rise causing jaundice of the skin. Jason began looking unhealthy. I was thankful to have the knowledge base to know what was going on. However, it was still hard to watch. Good open communication with the doctor is so important so you can discuss physical changes that you observe in your child between office visits. Never be afraid to ask questions of your doctor. The doctor is there to help both you and your child.

As Jason's liver and spleen enlarged, there was frequent reassurance needed about his appearance. He was looking somewhat like an old man with a prominent belly from too much beer. He said that kids at school told him he looked like he needed to go on a diet. As any good parent would in this case, I would point out positive things about how he looked and his personality. It is important when your child is expressing negative thoughts about their body image to keep open communication going. Try to help your child find something positive to focus on to help diminish the negative preoccupation with body image issues. Jason knew his stomach stuck out, but he wanted to hear me say he looked okay.

# An Outpouring of Love

Through the whole ordeal of Jason being listed for a liver transplant I will never forget Katie and George's role in this. Katie's son and Jason had been in school together since Kindergarten. Katie and I became close friends. George and I even coached the boys' basketball team for a couple of years. George and my husband went to college together. Katie and George started a webpage for Jason called liverforjason.com. She also printed a flyer about Jason's story and his need for a transplant. This couple and the school's ministry to my family was such a blessing. Our church also got behind Jason's need for a liver transplant. The pastor announced this in the sanctuary during church service. Flyers were also given out to all those entering the church sanctuary one Sunday morning. We had meals and prayers and hospital visits from school friends and church friends for a few months.

A school contact who owned a Christian radio station put Jason's need for a liver transplant on one of the Christian radio stations. Neither my husband nor I could be donors. This was due to an elevated liver enzyme that we both had, and the amount of liver tissue required for transplantation in a child Jason's size. The web page, the flyers, and the Christian radio station made Jason's need known. Even a special phone line in the transplant office was set up for Jason because there were so many people trying to donate some of their liver to Jason. The outpouring of love was overwhelming.

# Jason Gets a Call for a Liver

Jason got a call for a liver, but the first call didn't materialize into a transplant. He had a fever and could not undergo surgery. We were so disappointed. Had we missed the therapeutic window? Could Jason get well enough to undergo surgery?

A week later he got another call for a liver transplant and this call materialized on Easter weekend. He had a transplant. The doctor said it was a very good match! I will always remember those families at the Christian school that both boys attended. They were wonderful to us during Jason's long-term battle with liver disease and later his liver transplantation. Chase and I can never thank Katie and George enough for spear-heading the movement in the community to help with Jason's transplantation.

Right before Jason's liver transplant at age sixteen, the hepatologist asked Jason if there was anything that he wanted to ask him before surgery. Jason wanted to know if he could take his liver, after it was taken out, to his biology class and show his class. The doctor politely said no that was not possible, but he was quite amused by Jason's question. He did tell Jason that after his liver was removed, he would arrange to show his liver to his parents. The hepatologist kept his promise. In an anteroom right outside the operating room the liver doctor showed us Jason's huge scarred liver in a sterile basin. The scarred liver looked like it had a bunch of golf balls all over it. It was all knotty and had very irregular shape around its edges. We took a picture of it and showed it to Jason sometime after his surgery. He took this picture to his biology class to show them. Jason's liver was approximately two times the size of a normal liver. No wonder, Jason's abdomen protruded as his liver disease advanced.

# After Liver Transplantation

When Jason was wheeled into ICU after having his liver transplant, he looked amazing. He no longer was jaundice(yellow). His color was so healthy looking. He no longer had a protruding abdomen. He did have a mesh covering over his abdomen, because the liver was too large at that time to completely close the abdomen. The new liver had to shrink down, so to speak, and adapt to Jason's abdominal size. It was good the surgeon couldn't close completely because Jason developed a biliary leak a few days post op that needed to be surgically corrected. At nine days post operatively, his abdomen was completely closed, and the mesh was no longer needed. He responded amazing well to this new organ that he was so graciously given. I remember a few days after surgery, when Jason got a side view of himself in the mirror. I quite vividly remember that moment when Jason could see that his stomach didn't stick out anymore. He shed a few tears of joy and expressed relief in knowing that now he looked like everyone else.

We went back for follow-up visits at the liver transplant clinic post operatively. I remember when one of the transplant PAs took out Jason's abdominal staples and commented to Jason that he looked "awesome." All members of the liver transplant team were wonderful. It seemed that every one of them knew just what to say to us when Jason and I both needed a little encouragement. We had frequent visits at the liver transplant clinic to check blood levels and adjust Jason's anti-rejection medications. The steroids he was given for quite a while impacted his diabetes, making the diabetes harder to control. This was a process we had to monitor. As time went on, his anti-rejection medicines were decreased. He began gaining some weight and looking more filled out.

I can't say enough positive things about the liver transplant team at the local children's hospital. They were so knowledgeable and skilled at their craft. I will always remember the compassion we were showed from this group of medical professionals. I especially appreciated how personal the liver transplant surgeon was. He had an excellent reputation regarding surgical skill. He also had an excellent bedside manner and a very cute sense of humor. The whole team had a very upbeat attitude which eased our anxiety throughout the whole liver transplant process

As soon as Jason came home from the hospital he wanted to go to his high school. He wanted to say hello to his friends and thank them for pulling for him during transplant. He received accolades of praise on his return to school. He was beaming with pride one day after school when he said that he had a lot of status now at school. I was not quite sure what this meant, but he was getting a lot of positive vibes from all his classmates. Jason missed a ton of school that year, but they allowed him to advance to the next grade. He was fearful that, because of his illness and transplant, he would not be able to graduate with his friends. This was truly a gift to advance with his peers.

# The Need to Reboot

I was exhausted! I was in full blown menopause during all the liver transplant ordeal with some sleeping difficulties too. I needed to reboot emotionally and physically right after Jason's liver transplant. My body seemed to know that we were somewhat over the most serious health crisis of Jason and in a quasi-safe zone, so to speak. Jason's doctor firmly recommended that I go home from the hospital and get some needed rest in my own bed. I had to take three or four days of rest and recuperation the week after Jason's liver transplant. I had to do this before I went back to the hospital to stay with him. I remember back to that time, now, as to why I wore out. For ten months before Jason's liver transplant he was going into the hospital twice a month. When he was discharged home, he was getting IVs during the night that I often was administering through home health equipment. The liver transplant was more taxing than I realized. However, my doctor could wisely see this and knew what I needed to do. My family was great at that time taking turns staying with Jason while I recouped. Even my cousins, who lived in town, took a turn staying with Jason while I took a few nights of sleep at home.

Mothers always think they can endure most anything when it comes to taking care of their child's needs. During that time period though, I took some medication for a while to help me sleep. I knew I needed to get some sleep so I could more effectively take care of Jason's health needs. I made sure to get some walk/jog activity in the garden area at the hospital when I could. Once we got back home, I tried to get back into the running routine. Exercise became a great outlet and stress reliever for me during the intense times of Jason's illness. I just needed to try and set aside a little time to do this. Mothers, as best as you can, keep an eye on your own physical and emotional energy.

# My Husband's Business
# Hits Rock Bottom

Life happens right? But why did we have to go through tremendous financial pressure on top of everything else? For right about ten years, the building business really slowed down. My husband came close to losing his business. I left my private practice and went to work full-time at the university to get health insurance benefits for my family. One month before our insurance premium was going up to $4,000.00 dollars a month, I accepted a fulltime position as a college professor at a local university. What a relief to get a break on insurance by working for a large university. We also had to take a second mortgage out on our house to help pay for kids' college. The medical bills were huge which zapped our financial resources. This was another unpleasant situation my family was forced to cope with. Somehow, we managed to pull through. We still have some financial recovery to do, like a lot of families do, when a child becomes seriously ill.

# Jason Is Going to College
# but with Oxygen

I never thought Jason would be able to leave home and go to college. I remember meeting with disability services at the college to get him special accommodations like a single room, so he could do his aerosol treatments privately. I wanted to get him on ground floor, so he would not have to walk up so many flights of steps each day.

Up to that point, we had never sought out disability services for anything. However, Jason let me know he was not going to have anything to do with disability services. Jason wanted to be like all the other college students. So he went through being in a fraternity and having roommates. He was the favorite pledge of the fraternity that year. The experience of being in a fraternity, and living away from home, did wonders for Jason's self-concept and independence. He and his fraternity brothers are still close today. Some of his fraternity brothers even made a few trips to see Jason around his lung transplant time.

When you can't change your situation, try to change your perspective on how you view things. I have said this very often to patients struggling with difficult situations. I work to try to help them look at alternatives to the problems they are facing. I have learned that looking at alternatives puts one in a more active phase of problem solving. I think this helps individuals move from a passive to active phase and provides some semblance of control.

I followed my own advice when changing my perspective about Jason's college years with oxygen. Rather than having a pity party, when other parents talked about their child's college experience, I thought about Jason's predicted life expectancy. I thought, well going to college with oxygen certainly beats the neonatologist's prediction that Jason would only live to be ten.

It seems that Jason's lungs were deteriorating at a rapid rate during college. His doctors and I talked about this. Is it that when kids leave the oversight of their parents, they become less conscientious about their healthcare when they go off to school? That may be partially true, but college age is also a time when the CF disease may advance more rapidly on its own.

Jason's lung function began to severely deteriorate during these years. He had to withdraw from two different semesters due to extended hospitalization for repeated lung infections. Dropping classes was becoming more frequent and necessary for Jason to remain in school. Just being able to walk to classes and keep schoolwork up was growing more difficult.

Each year of the first four years of college became more difficult for Jason than the previous one. When Jason would get lung infections and go on IV steroids his blood sugar would spike. Monitoring his diabetes was difficult with the steroids. He was functioning with about forty percent lung function around this time. Life was hard for Jason with this diminished lung capacity with just the routine activities of being a college student. It was hard as a parent seeing Jason's life be such a struggle. Jason's perseverance to want to graduate from college was quite admirable in my eyes. He was so determined to stay in school and graduate, until he just couldn't do it anymore. I remember the day Jason called me and said he needed to come home. We had an understanding that Jason would let me know when he felt like he couldn't live away from home and be a college student. He came home and took one semester of school at a local four-year college. It was easier on him not having to worry about meals or any of his home care needs. When lung numbers dropped to thirty his CF doctor said it was time to consider lung transplantation. Finally, we took a complete break from college to move toward a lung transplant.

We trusted the guidance our CF doctor gave us. He was beyond exceptional in our opinion. This CF doctor had taken over Jason's care when Jason had just turned twelve years of age. He treated Jason through his mid-twenties until his lung transplant at twenty-five.

This doctor had a wonderful way of relating to CF teens and young adults. He had long hair, wore blue jeans, a rugged sport coat and very colorful ties. Every tie he wore had a special history that he would tell us about. He played rock music back in the exam room area. He would talk to the teens about the music that was playing and have a conversation about what music Jason liked while he examined him. He was the type of doctor most young adults would love to sit down and chat with over a beer.

Jason's move back home was needed, but hard for him psychologically. I don't think any adult child after they have lived independently is happy about moving under their parents' roof again. At least this was the way my two boys felt. We had to make some modifications for Jason when he moved back home. We had to change things like putting a refrigerator in his room to keep drinks and his medication supplies that needed refrigerating. Walking to the kitchen to get food and drinks was a lot of unnecessary effort for Jason. We also put a portable air conditioning unit in his room, to keep it extra cool during the summer months even though we had central air conditioning.

Jason was down and out with his limited lung capacity. He thought a dog would brighten his spirits. Jason wanted another golden retriever like the two we had when he was growing up. This might not have been the best move at the time, but we did it anyway. I thought maybe this would boost Jason's spirits. He bought Berkley. It ended up though, that with Jason being so sick most of the dog care fell to me and my husband. The dog did give Jason something else to focus on besides his difficulty breathing, but it was hard for him to care for her. She was a lot to handle and still is at five years of age. Jason, to this day, still remembers the day his dog Berkley ran across the street ready to plow down a very fragile grandmother of our next-door neighbor. He had to sprint across the street on less than thirty percent lung function. Jason said he could see the grandmother headed for a serious fall. He managed to grab Berkley just in time. Jason said it took him most of the afternoon to recover from this exertion.

One day Jason stated adamantly that he was tired of having no life and not being able to do things. He went on to say that he was definitely ready to pursue a lung transplant. Jason became a strong advocate for his care. He researched hospitalized and decided that Duke was the place for us to go. They were doing one hundred and fifty transplants a year with good statistics and survival rate. My husband and I agreed with Jason's decision. It was indeed time to look at lung transplantation.

# We Started Transplant Visits at Duke

W e started regular visits at Duke every three months for a full three-year period. Jason and I would travel up to Duke for two to three days of tests and appointments. My husband and I had to alternate taking turns because of our job responsibilities. Our general impression of the transplant doctors and medical staff was excellent. Everyone there seemed so knowledgeable and encouraging. They checked everything out on Jason. They even checked things out on me as the primary care giver for Jason. He and I both had to undergo some psychological testing of sorts to see if we were good candidates for lung transplantation. In my previous job as a heart transplant psychologist I was familiar with most of the tests administered to us by the lung transplant psychologist. I thought it was a very good idea to check out the care giver's mental health stability along with the transplant candidate's stability.

The trips became taxing and harder on Jason. His energy level was getting more diminished, as each week passed. We met several post lung transplant patients during those three month-check-ups. It was very encouraging to see young adults who looked like people with CF who looked pretty good. Of course, we also saw lung transplant patients who did not look very good. After tracking Jason's lung function and overall declining health condition for over two years, the lung transplant team felt it was time for us to relocate to Durham, North Carolina. We relocated as close to Duke hospital as we could in a two-bedroom apartment and began the lung transplant process.

# We Moved to Durham, North Carolina

I took family medical leave from the university where I taught as well as the ten weeks of vacation I had accrued. I had been with the University System of Georgia for several years by then. My husband traveled every weekend to come see us. He kept working during the week. Times were still very slow in the building business, but it seemed to be showing some signs of improvement. My family was on my insurance plan with the university, so that was very good, thank the Lord. Double lung transplants are not cheap. We also had the expense of relocation to an apartment in Durham, North Carolina near Duke hospital.

We were not able to take Berkley, Jason's golden retriever, with us. She still had too much puppy in her then for us to manage with everything else going on with Jason at that time. Through a church friend we found a couple who loved goldens and was willing to keep Jason's golden for several months. It turned out, by more than coincidence, that the husband of this couple had had a double lung transplant a year and a half prior. They wanted to give back to others for all the things people had done for them during lung transplant. What a bonding experience we had with Susan and Dave. They are wonderful people. We continue to stay in touch with them today. They invited us to Dave's five-year anniversary of his lung transplant. They celebrated his lung anniversary with a cookout with family and friends. I remember the cute cake for Dave that was shaped like two lungs. We were happy to be invited to this celebration.

# Lots of Physical Therapy and Conditioning

After we moved to Durham Jason had to participate in several weeks of physical therapy and education classes. This was a requirement before he could be listed for a lung transplant. Five days a week, he had physical therapy and some educational classes with other transplant candidates in the waiting phase. This went on for about six weeks. The goal of physical therapy before lung transplant was to build up the individual as much as possible before surgery. Also, psychologically I was told, this was important to check for patient perseverance and determination. At least two months of physical therapy was also required every day post-transplant. This had to happen before a patient was discharged back to their permanent home.

Along with this training, Jason had transplant clinic visits once to twice a week with different transplant team doctors and other professional transplant staff. We felt somewhat like a hamster on a circular wheel, repeating the same thing every day. At the end of Jason's six weeks of physical therapy pre-transplant he was given a certificate of completion to this first phase of treatment. He was then listed on the transplant list for Duke Medical Center.

There was a treadmill in the apartment complex we rented. The apartment was very close to the place Jason had physical therapy. While Jason was in physical therapy, the treadmill and I had a two-hour date. So I would run, walk and get some needed exercise. Man, this really helped my head. Otherwise, Jason and I just hung out together at the apartment. Jason still needed continuous oxygen. We eventually got a huge oxygen tank that we nicknamed R2D2O2 after the Star Wars character. We watched a ton of Netflix shows and kept up with Duke basketball on TV. I read more books than I have ever read at one time. Jason was an avid reader and writer as well. He wrote a lot of his Caring Bridge posts before his transplant.

I need to put in a good word for my dog Bear. He was a great diversion for us in the apartment. He also was my bed companion while Chase was back at home. He was two years old and all of ten pounds. He simply loved the apartment because he got so much attention from us. Jason and I enjoyed petting and playing with him. It helped pass some of the boredom of waiting for a transplant. I remember when the weather got cold, one of my sources of amusement was dressing him out in different winter sweaters. I would take pictures of him in his sweaters and text them to friends. There wasn't much else positive to text home about during the waiting phase.

A few family and friends traveled all the way to North Carolina to visit us while we waited for a set of lungs. We were far away from our normal support system of friends and family. But as time went by, we developed some close relationships with other people who also were waiting for lung transplants. I remember so vividly the older couple who lived immediately across from us at the apartment complex. They were so kind and thoughtful. They had been waiting longer than we had. They gave us the lowdown on things we needed to know. I think our neighbor's wife was central in arranging the Friday lunches for caregivers. These lunch meetings served as a great resource of information. Also, while we were waiting for transplant, there were a couple of large nice dinner gatherings for the transplant candidates and their caregivers. Duke's program had provided the opportunity for a great sense of comradery among the people waiting for lung transplants.

Our neighbor at the apartment use to kid me about being from the south. He and his wife were from up north. When Jason had a few bad days in a row he brought us a bucket of Kentucky Fried Chicken in honor of our southern roots. All the transplant patients were very good at trying to encourage one another to hang in there. Our apartment neighbors were like adopted parents to me. They seemed to look out for me and Jason. One day, when the delivery for

Jason's tank of oxygen was late, our neighbor let us have some of his spare oxygen until our delivery came. We grew to love them.

Jason and I tried to do things on the weekend to break up the monotony of the "WAIT." We tried going to the movies with portable oxygen. The second time was a disaster. The movie ran over time and Jason's oxygen ran out. I am surprised I didn't get a ticket rushing home to get him hooked up to his oxygen tank at the apartment. Not getting enough oxygen is most anxiety producing, to say the least. I would call it true panic. We did venture out for short breaks to go out to eat carrying plenty of portable oxygen.

The friendships and bonding I developed at the Friday caregiver lunches were very helpful to me. I got to talk with other caregivers about how they were coping with the transplant wait for their loved ones. Jason also developed a good bit of comradery with the other pretransplant patients in physical therapy and the transplant education classes.

# Struggling to Keep Weight Up

Jason lost weight because it took so many calories for him just to breathe. He watched movies, read books, and rested. He stayed fatigued much of the time. If he lost too much weight, he would fall out-of-range for a transplant. I cooked anything and everything he might like, but he couldn't eat much at one time and had little interest in food. The site of too much food on his plate made him feel sick. We quickly reverted to the small frequent feedings recommended for people with advanced lung disease. He also drank boost twice a day to increase calorie intake. Psychologically, this waiting was emotionally and physically exhausting for Jason. He had been a trooper all his life. I prayed, for him to make it through this hurdle.

Jason ended up having to go on tube feedings through a "GJ" tube to keep from losing any more weight. This was not pleasant for him, but a necessity if he was going to qualify for transplant. He lost down to one hundred eight pounds on his five-foot-seven frame. This was as low as he could go. He had the best nutritionist. I can still see this little four-foot-eleven cute young woman motivating Jason. She was amazing, and so very smart too. At each visit she always seemed to have new suggestions for us to try and bump up calorie intake.

When Baker came up to visit us one weekend, Jason got a call for a transplant. We rushed around as quickly as we could grabbing up the prepacked bags we had. Baker drove us there. We didn't get very far though. We got another call saying it was not a good match. We never made it to the hospital before we were told it was a no-go. That was quite a downer. We understood this could happen often with a potential transplant call that may not materialize for a variety of different reasons. In our education classes about transplantation, we learned that it was not uncommon to have false calls. The transplant team referred to these calls as "dry runs." A dry run call meant that, for one reason or another, the organ was not going to be a good match for the recipient.

# We Get the Real Call for Transplant

I remember the weekend we got the REAL CALL. Chase told me he wasn't going to come that weekend because he had been quite busy during the past few work weeks and needed to take a break from the trip. I completely understood but we would miss his visit. At that time my older son Baker was living at home with Chase for a while after grad school while Jason and I lived in Durham. Being split up was hard on the family. We lived like this for a full eight months. Well, something changed Chase's mind at the last minute. He surprised us and showed up any way that weekend. This turned out to be a real blessing, too. That Saturday evening, right after Jason took a shower, we got a transplant call. It was just in the nick of time. Jason had been on ten liters of oxygen and still struggling to breathe. His chest was barrel looking from his prolonged lung disease. He looked emaciated and thoroughly exhausted from expending energy to take a shower. I really didn't think he could get any thinner or sustain himself much longer in this physical condition. As he was laying on the sofa recovering from his shower, we got a call to come to the hospital for a transplant. It was unusual for all three of us to be together on the sofa because Jason spent the vast majority of his day and evening lying in bed exhausted. I will never forget the moment Chase's phone rang telling us to come to the hospital. I think for a moment we must have been in a state of shock. Nobody moved for a few seconds. We then jumped excitedly into high gear. We grabbed our things and off we drove to Duke.

The car ride to Duke was filled with a lot of nervous chatter. We wondered if this would be another dry run transplant call or if it was going to be the real deal. With this call we made it all the way to the hospital. After being admitted, we waited for about three hours or so in a special type of preop room. If Jason got the go for transplant the hospital staff would put a red sterile head cap on him. A few more minutes passed and then a staff member came into our room with a red cap. Hallelujah, Jason had a red cap put on his head. He got the go for transplant. The surgeon thereafter came to talk with Chase and me about how long the surgery would probably take.

Chase and I stayed in a waiting area all night and through the next morning. Jason's brother arrived from Atlanta early that morning having hit the road driving shortly after we called him. All I remember about waiting at the hospital during the lung transplant was that it was freezing. We had no blankets or pillows. We just huddled up together on a sofa trying to stay warm. They probably told us in the pretransplant classes to bring a blanket and some pillows, but I must have forgotten about that part of our teaching. If there is ever a next time, I will remember to bring a blanket. I'm just saying.

I think the surgery took about ten hours as best as we can remember. It started at 1:00 a.m. on Sunday morning and finished at 11:00 a.m. The surgeon came to talk with us after the surgery and said that Jason had a very good match. He said the lungs fit just perfectly into Jason's chest. This was music to our ears. We knew nothing about the donor but were humbled by this gift of life.

When we got to see Jason in the intensive care unit, he was intubated with a respirator connected to him. He had multiple IVs and various tubes attached to him. What I noticed right off the bat was his excellent color. He no longer looked an ashen color or was struggling to breath. I saw on his hospital monitor that his oxygen saturation was an awesome 100 percent on room air. He only stayed intubated a few hours. I do remember something funny Jason did while we were in the ICU with him. He was awake but his hands and legs were restrained. He could not talk because of the tube in his throat. He was trying to tell me something. But when I couldn't understand him, he shot me a bird. Yes, he shot me a bird. Later after his breathing tube was taken out, I found out what this was about. He said his ear was really itching and he couldn't scratch it because of the restraints on his hands. He was frustrated because I couldn't understand what he needed. I got a good chuckle out of this.

When my husband and I got a good look at each other in the ICU, after seeing Jason, we squeezed our hands together tight. We knew right then and there that we had just witnessed a major miracle. God is good. God is miraculous!

# Right after Lung Transplant

At the end of the first day after Jason was transplanted, the nurses had him up walking. I couldn't believe what I was seeing. The physical therapists and transplant doctors had stressed to Jason before surgery how important it was for him to get upright and walking as soon as possible to help the new lungs. The transplant team referred to this as important "Reebok Therapy." They emphasized this so much to Jason that the first question out of his mouth to the ICU nurse was "When can I walk?" I think it took about three people walking with him to push along all his IV poles and other things he needed connected to him while he took a loop around the nurses' station.

I was impressed with how skilled and compassionate the ICU nurses were in their care of Jason. Three times a day he would walk around the nurse's station. The doctors indicated he set a record with his diligence in getting up and moving. Each time he walked he would increase the number of laps. He was so committed to doing well back then and now.

There were several things that were tough after transplant. One was the frequent bronchoscopy (inserting a tube down your throat to inspect the airways in the lungs). At the same time, usually a biopsy was done to take tissue samples to check for rejection. This was a very important and necessary procedure, but I understand it is uncomfortable to have to go through.

Jason was tested for gastric reflux several times during this hospitalization. This was a very unpleasant procedure for Jason. We were told gastric reflux was a common source of getting food particles in the lungs which could set up a media for infection. If you recall, a feeding tube (called a GJ tube) was inserted in Jason's stomach before transplant to receive nourishment when his weight dropped too low. This feeding tube was now used after transplant until Jason could safely eat by mouth. The transplant team was very careful to make sure Jason would not aspirate any food contents into his lungs through gastric reflux.

Jason had five chest tubes, two large bandages on his side, a "GJ" feeding tube and a line of surgical staples horizontally across his breastbone where the surgeon closed him postoperatively. Jason looked like he had been worked over pretty well by this point. But he gladly took this to be able to breathe on his own. Day by day his strength started improving. His morale also was good. It was hard not to be positive about all the transplant maintenance procedures with such a warm, upbeat and supportive transplant team. My family can't say enough positive comments about the whole experience of lung transplantation at Duke. Everyone there was so encouraging, knowledgeable, and professional.

After a month, Jason was discharged to go back home to the apartment in Durham. He was transplanted on January twenty-five, but we had to stay in Durham until the very end of April. There was still much to be done after Jason left the hospital. He had a good eight weeks of physical therapy at the transplant physical therapy workout center. The staff there was like everyone else related to the lung transplant team. They were very encouraging, knowledgeable and professional.

Jason made a lot of friends through this center. The contacts he made were people about his age as well as some older individuals waiting for lung transplant. There were a variety of reasons the individuals we met needed a lung transplant. The younger ones though were most often waiting because of things like advancing CF disease. I became close to a couple of mothers who had daughter's with CF waiting for transplant.

Along with the daily conditioning program we had to follow up weekly with the doctors, nutritionist and various other important transplant staff. Jason had weekly then monthly bronchoscopies. When we left Duke and moved back home, we had to return very often for check-up that first year. Now that Jason lives in Birmingham, he follows up with the lung and liver transplant doctors at the University of Alabama Medical Center in Birmingham.

# Rebounding

I think about both of my boys and often think how they are my inspiration in life. Both Jason and Baker have overcome so many health challenges and made adaptations to keep living life to the fullest. This has inspired me beyond words. I remember vividly Baker's success in sports and academics after a rug, so to speak, was pulled quickly out from under him at age ten. Sometimes I think it may be harder to bounce back from something medically when you have experienced optimal life before the illness. I will never forget my family's rejoicing three years after Baker lost his colon to be undefeated in his wrestling season in eighth grade. He was quite the fighter. He rebounded well enough after his colectomy to regain his status as a good athlete during his middle and high school years. He is still quite the athlete today.

I remember back to the image of Jason struggling to breathe before transplant even on oxygen. But then I think about Jason and his first six-mile road race just eight months after his lung transplant. It was a cystic fibrosis race that we ran together. Chase was our biggest supporter as he enthusiastically cheered us on. Then, later on that first year after lung transplant, Jason did a ten-mile race and half marathon with me and Chase. Who would have ever thought Jason would have been able to accomplish this endeavor? My family, beyond a shadow of a doubt, has learned to capitalize on the good times in life. For us, we just sometimes had to endure a lot of the not so good times to get there.

# Marital Strain

So many times I have counseled with couples who have a child with special health or emotional needs of some sort. The child's special needs can put a significant amount of stress on the marriage and the family. The child can easily become the central focus of everyday living. But all relationships within the family need to be nurtured as best you can, depending on the level of immediate stress of the child's health problem. A strong marital relationship and communication is important to the family. When stresses on the family are great, children need to see the parents working as a team and sharing the load. Did my husband and I always agree on how to address our children's physical and emotional needs? Absolutely not, but we worked on it and kept communicating about the problems we were facing. A couple of times we sought some professional counseling to help us problem solve some tough spots as a couple and as a family. But it was our commitment to each other that kept us together. I recently heard a pastor at a wedding say that in life the feelings of love can change but the *promise* to love lasts forever." We are now in our thirty-fifth year of marriage. We would both agree that we are very happily married

It may be your pastor, a very close family member, a psychologist or other trained professional who may be helpful for you to talk with when stresses with your child are great. But since I am in the field of counseling, I want to point out that all therapists are not equal. Look at their professional credentials and experience in dealing with families with health crises. I have always said to my clients that therapists are kind of like a pair of new shoes. Sometimes you try on a couple of pairs before you find the right fit for you.

# Jason Gets Squamous Cell Skin Cancer

Just when you think everything is running so smoothly a little bump in the road happens. Jason developed skin cancer. According to what we learned at the transplant clinic in Durham, transplant patients are at a high risk of having squamous cell skin cancer. We met a few other patients in Durham that shared this experience with us. Jason's dermatologist told him that this is related to the immunosuppressant drugs that transplant patients take to avoid rejection. It also is related to the fact that they are organ recipients. Jason developed squamous cell skin cancer as a result of this. He had been following up with dermatology at least every six months since lung transplantation. He had two spots on his head biopsied and both came back squamous cell. Right after graduation from nursing school he had Mohs surgery to remove both cancers on his scalp. Fortunately, all the cancer was able to be excised. The dermatology group emphasized to Jason that he needed to continue to follow with every three to six months dermatology checkups because of the increased risk for him to have other skin cancers.

Jason's brother Baker was most helpful when Jason was worried that his head would be disfigured from the Mohs skin cancer surgery. My understanding was a conversation like this. Baker told Jason that dude, you have enough things trying to kill you so don't worry about a little skin cancer. Baker went on to say that Jason could always get a toupee if it really bothered him that much. Anyway, Baker's big-brother love and typical practical approach to things was very helpful to Jason at that point in time. The dermatologist was able to extract all the cancer which we were all very pleased about.

# Resilience

How important is optimism, happiness, and vitality to one's well-being? Positive psychology theory believes that it is very important. I incorporate a good bit of positive psychology in my practice in counseling with clients and find it helpful. On a personal note, my husband and I tried to make our family life as normal and as positive as we could. At times we might have tried too hard. We worked to have as many joyous times around the physical limitations Jason had and the health challenges Baker had at one time. We strove to promote their independence and capitalized on the things they could do. We made many mistakes along the way, but we tried to do our best as parents. I remember what one of the boy's doctors told me about the health challenges they both had to face. This wise pediatrician said that each boy would have to learn to make the most of what he has. Now, as I reflect back on that advice, I think, shouldn't we all go through life like that anyway?

# My Regrets

I regret the times I needed to focus intently on Jason's medical needs during some critical times in Baker's life, specifically during Baker's high school and early college years. This was a time when Jason was very sick. I once asked Baker what it was like to have a brother who was critically ill. Baker told me that it was awful. Baker said that he didn't know if Jason was going to live or die. Baker went on to describe that almost every time he called home when he was away at college Jason was always getting sicker and Dad's business was getting ready to crumble. Baker commented that at that time in his life he needed to be away from home to kind of protect him from all that bad news with his family.

Baker wanted to go far away to school for college, and I understand many of his reasons why. During Baker's senior year of high school Jason had his liver transplant. This was a time of great joy and happiness for Baker, but things were not calm around our house. I remember scheduling college visits with Baker around when Jason was not in the hospital. I felt that Baker was out of the spotlight so to speak with his accomplishments at that time in his life. I wished things had been different for him as he prepared to leave home and go away to college. I did not get to spend as much individual time with Baker his senior year because of Jason's repeated hospitalizations right before his liver transplant. I wished I could have cloned myself then and spent needed individual time with each boy. This wasn't possible and I still have my regrets about Baker's senior year.

Baker chose Baylor University in Texas where one of his cousins lived. He loved his school and fell in love with Texas. That is the problem with kids going far away from home to school. They end up liking the area where the school is located and want to stay near there. At least I have heard this from several other parents whose kids went to school far away from their parents' home. For Baker, he made a good choice for himself then, and now he lives in Texas. He has a very good job in Texas that his undergraduate work in biology at Baylor helped to prepare him. His graduate work at Notre Dame was in the business aspect of science. His current job suits him very well, and the Texas environment meets his social aspirations.

I always tried to give equal attention to both boys but sometimes as parents you just do the best you can. Try not to let guilt pull you down over this. The sickest child often requires your immediate attention and then some. Just make sure the other children know your love for them does not waiver during these times. When time permits and things are calm at home give the other children some special devoted attention.

# My Interview with Jason

I thought long and hard about how I wanted to include Jason's perspective on living with CF. He agreed to let me interview him. Here are the questions I asked him with his responses.

1. Question: Jason, do you remember at what age you understood what CF was and that you had it?
   Response: I remember having to do things that other kids didn't have to do at a young age. The earliest memory I have of breathing treatments was the elephant tube blowing steam in my face while I was watching Barney on TV. I don't think I knew the complexity of CF affecting my lungs and digestive tract until I was about six years old.

2. Question: What was it like being the only member in your family who had CF?
   Response: I felt like too much stuff revolved around my health. It was a topic I heard my mother and different family talk a lot about when I was little. There was too much emphasis placed on my health and how I was doing. I got tired of hearing people talk about it.

3. Question: At what point in your life do you remember your illness impacting you physically with physical limitations?
   Response: I was probably about ten or eleven years old when I noticed CF affecting me physically. I started slowing down in sports and having trouble catching my breath when I would be running. From the age of about ten years old until lung transplant my breathing problems just kept getting worse. My liver problems were getting worse about the same time too and that affected my endurance also. I

really did not like how my illness affected me with physical limitations, like in sports. Everybody else my age was growing, and I wasn't. I really didn't like not being able to compete in sports.

4. Question: At what point in your life did you notice CF affecting you socially with your peers?

   Response: Around the time of my liver transplant, I really noticed how CF impacted my relationship with my peers. I got to where I didn't have anything in common with my peers at school. I didn't see life from the same perspective as they did, especially after I was transplanted.

5. Question: What were the ongoing CF checkups like for you?

   Response: CF checkups were defeating. It was like there was a cloud over my head. I could do everything in my power to do things right and take care of myself. I could do my very best but still get put in the hospital. I think I had to learn then how to pick myself up when I got put down. It was defeating to try my best to stay healthy and still get put in the hospital by my CF doctor.

6. Question: Describe your experience with having to do breathing treatments every day until your lung transplant.

   Response: A big chunk of my day was tied up with breathing treatments. My first thought every morning was that I needed to do a breathing treatment. I would wake up congested from sleeping through the night with all the mucous collecting in my lungs. I would have to do treatments to get back to baseline which wasn't that great. But then as the day went on, I would get congested and need to do a breathing treatment by evening. At times, I would have to cut my breathing treatments short before school. I remember a lot of times I would go into school a little late because I needed to get a good breathing treatment in before I started the day.

7. Question: Did you ever blame your parents for your having CF?

Response: No. I do blame my parents for being short though.

8. Question: What is most memorable about how your parents raised you as a CF child?

Response: As a kid growing up, I was not sheltered. I was always encouraged to do things. Perseverance was huge for me. My parents were both doers, and they encouraged us to do stuff. You didn't shelter us. I was raised so normally that I didn't have as much in common with other CF kids growing up.

9. Question: What was it like going through a liver transplant?

Response: It was definitely encouraging to go through. It made me grow up quickly to be only sixteen years of age. I was grateful for what I did have. It made me think my peers were dumb and didn't really know about life. I just couldn't relate to them after that. During pretransplant you can really feel your body deteriorating. You kind of feel death staring at you in the face. I understood the gravity of it all. It was at the age I was driving. It was an odd age to have a liver transplant. I was just trying to be normal and live normal. The liver transplant helped me to be normal.

10. Question: What was it like going through a double lung transplant?

Response: Pretransplant was very hard. End stage lung disease was a lot harder than end stage liver disease for me. Oxygen was a leash. I was drowning in mucous and couldn't breathe. If I ate before breathing treatments, I would throw up my food. This happened more and more. The amount of time I could actually do something during the day was about five hours. Then I was in bed again. Oxygen was depressing and humbling. Going to the gym with oxygen was depressing. I just had to accept that I needed a lung transplant because my quality of life had gotten so much worse. I reverted back to no independence after living away at college and having to come back home to live. My friends from college were graduating, getting jobs and getting married. I couldn't plan for a future. I could only look a couple of days ahead. I checked out a good bit emotionally, and kind of went numb. There wasn't any excitement in my life. The transplant itself was tough! The first two weeks after transplant I felt like I was in the twilight zone. Once I finally got home after the transplant, I felt good. This was about two months or so. For the first time since I can remember, it became enjoyable not to have to work to breathe. Breathing for me became a passive act. I couldn't believe it after transplant. This felt amazing! It was like my hard drive had been changed. Everything was quick and fast to me now. After I was transplanted, and things were easier on me I realized how much I had accomplished with a bad set of lungs. I was proud of what I had been able to accomplish on what little lung function I had. What I hated about lung transplant were the chest tubes, the dry mouth and the bronchoscopies that really "sucked!"

11. Question: What advice would you give to a CF child and their parents?
    Response: I would tell them to be sure to stay active. Learn what your new normal is for you regarding your health. I would tell the parents not to shelter their child.

12. Question: How do you see your future now?
    Response: The way I look at my future depends on the day. Usually the day is good. However, sometimes I feel like a ticking time bomb if I plan too far ahead. Overall, I guess my future looks good. I still get frustrated with health stuff. I am cured of most of my health problems and the social aspect is easier. However, socially things are still somewhat difficult as a transplant individual.

# My Interview with Baker

1.  Question: Baker, you had an abrupt onset to your illness starting with a virus that basically ate up your colon. What was that like for you as a young child?

    Response: It was really bad! I didn't really understand how bad it was until later in life. I think a lot of the setbacks from the effects of a childhood illness show themselves more after puberty. At least it did for me anyway. When you are a kid you are taken care of a lot by your parents. It was hard for me to feel the full impact of my illness until about age fourteen. During my pre-illness years I was 90–95 percent good at everything. Post illness I had to work super hard at everything like sports and even academics to be 80–85 percent good at things. Interrupted sleep due to my illness affected me in far reaching ways regarding my performance at things.

2.  Question: What helped you cope during the weeks, months, and years of adjustment to having a colectomy?

    Response: What really helped was having family and close friends I could be honest with about what was going on with me. Close friends and family I could talk to about my intestinal problems was a big help. Also, I learned tips along the way that helped me cope just by living day to day with my illness.

3.  Question: How do you manage not having a colon in your daily life now?

    Response: I am pretty meticulous about trying to stay on a healthy diet. If I eat really badly my bowels will let me know it. I have learned to adapt to the frequent discomfort of having diarrhea. You learn to deal as best you can with what you have.

4. Question: What was most memorable about how your parents cared for you during the weeks and months after your surgery?

    Response: One thing that really helped me was that I knew my parents were always there for me. They always supported me in whatever way I needed. When I was younger, they took control of all the things they anticipated I needed without me having to give it much thought. They did a good job anticipating my daily needs.

5. Question: How do you see your future now?

    Response: My future is fine. It is good. My future is what I make of it. I realize the older I get the more I realize that people have setbacks in life. Setbacks along the line of something like what I experienced. People with setbacks in life just have to learn to cope and deal with it the best way they can.

6. Question: What would you like to share with parents of a child who has been diagnosed with ulcerative colitis?

    Response: I would encourage parents after their child had major surgery, to focus as the best they can, on controlling the child's symptoms. I encourage parents to help their child through good hydration, healthy diet and develop an overall healthy lifestyle including exercise. I believe it is important to control general stress as much as possible. I think the relationship between how stress impacts the bowels is not considered enough. Trying to help your child control general stress is good to do. I also want to emphasize how important it is to consider how interrupted sleep of being awakened four times a night to go to the bathroom affects the child's performance.

7. Question: What is it like being the only family member who had ulcerative colitis and required a colectomy?

    Response: I really never felt that set apart from the rest of the family with my bowel problems because Jason had so many problems in this area too. The family seemed to know how to deal with the awkwardness of talking about bowel function. Sometimes it felt like a fairly routine matter of conversation at my house.

# Jason's Career

After Jason's lung transplant, he finished the last bit of his college biology degree. He took a full-time job doing research at the Veteran's Affairs Hospital (VA) in Birmingham, Alabama and lived there with his golden retriever dog, Berkley. He then decided to enroll in the University of Alabama at Birmingham BSN Nursing Program. He started working part time while in school. He graduated from the nursing program at UAB in April 2019 and passed his nursing board exam. He then started his job as an RN in an inpatient psychiatric unit. This was a well thought out job position. As a transplant patient, Jason does not need to expose himself to unnecessary germs and disease. In inpatient psychiatry, where he works, the patients are medically stable with no physical needs for health care. This is a safer nursing environment for Jason to work in as a transplant individual.

# Baker's Career

Baker has always been very science-minded. His undergraduate degree in Biology from Baylor and graduate degree in a science business program from Notre Dame prepared him well for his current career with cardiac pacemakers. He is with a fast pace medical pacemaker company in Texas and very pleased with this position. He is meticulous about good diet and adequate fluid hydration to keep him functioning his best physically and mentally. He also knows to make sure he gets adequate hours of sleep. I have come to the realization that he now sees Texas as a state where he will probably stay.

# A Summary of Some Coping Thoughts

Through my years of experience as both an inpatient psychologist and registered nurse, I have a unique exposure to the mind body connection in coping with illness. I have always asked in the initial interview with clients what helped them cope with stressful events in the past. I want to find out what helped them get through tough times successfully. I know that how one coped with stressful events in the past helps to predict future adaptation. As you are faced with your child's diagnosis you will be challenged to call on previous positive coping strategies to help you through some tough times. I believe often an individual can get preoccupied with what stresses them and lose sight of what things help them cope.

I know how easy it is to focus on short comings. It is saddening to see the physical and or emotional limitations in your child. But this is a time your child needs you to focus on what they can do not what they can't. They need you to be their rock of stability as they come face to face with the limitations their illness brings. Try to help your child maximize what they can do to the fullest capacity. Revel in their accomplishments and goals they can achieve. I say this no matter what limitations they may be faced to live with. Don't lose focus on what positive things help both you and your child cope and be happy. I am not saying it will be easy. God knows it won't be. But I do know that a positive outlook is a powerful thing. In my work as a psychologist I know that our thoughts influence our actions, but our actions can also influence our thoughts. Remember this when you help your child move and do whatever activities they can.

As a parent of two children with chronic illnesses, I know it is painful to come face to face with the fact that your child does have limitations due to their medical diagnosis. But don't miss out on maximizing what abilities your child does have. I am always amazed at what feats a child can achieve when given consistent and strong genuine encouragement. I have seen this happen with both of my children. It is almost instinctive for parents to always want the very best for their child. No parent wants their child to suffer. I do believe it is possible to be realistic about your child's health problems and hopeful at the same time. I have always been taught in my training that hope is one of the single most important survival skills. I claimed this survival skill many times over with both my boys' illnesses.

Raising my two children with serious health problems was difficult and at times overwhelming beyond what words can express. As I think back to the very difficult years, there were three basic psychological factors that I held onto that help play an important role in a person's coping. These three basic factors that helped me through the ongoing stresses of my journey with my children's health issues were adequate information, social support, and sense of control.

When I talk about adequate information, I had to fully understand what my child's diagnosis was. What did this diagnosis implicate and what were the immediate needs of my child? I learned as much information as I could about each child's diagnosis and ongoing health status as their disease advanced. I read as much as I could about each child's illness. I asked as many questions of the physicians and health care team until I felt fully equipped as best as possible in understanding what challenges and limitations my child was facing at that moment. I know when things are just too painful to accept, it is easy to want to be like an ostrich and put your head in the sand and shut things out. Parents, if you can, try not to do this. Take your time to grieve over the disappointing news you have been given about your child. Talk this through with your spouse, a close family member, a dear friend, your pastor or a trained mental health professional. Do this so you can move forward and equip yourself with accurate information about your child's illness. Accurate information will help you more successfully problem solve. Correct information will help you make better decisions about your child's care. Make sure that you have access to good medical advice through well-trained physicians. Parents, it is also important to make sure your physician is experienced with your child's type of illness. Work on a good communication relationship with your child's physician and health care team. There may be one health team member with whom you have better communication. Access them as much as you can to give you the professional support you need.

Next, I advise parents to rally their support system. Parents may find it difficult to support their child if their own needs for support are not met. The parent can transmit their anxiety on to the child, who then may become more anxious. Identify family, friends, neighbors, your child's school representatives, community resources, and professionals whom you know you can call on when the need arises. This health journey, especially if it is chronic, may be like a marathon. You never want to deplete your personal resources too soon in the race. If you are not one to ask others for help, my advice is to try to get over this. You are most likely going to need to ask for some help from others. This is not a sign of weakness but often a sign of wisdom and astuteness. Sometimes you may just need a little help from your friends.

In addition to the stressors that are experienced with having a seriously ill child, parents may also have the dilemma of arranging care for the other children in the home. Other children at home will want and need parental attention as well. Warm parent-child relations within the family can help buffer the stress of having a chronically ill child in the home. A warm and caring explanation of the condition of the ill sibling should be carefully explained to the healthy children at an age appropriate level. The parents are a very vital component in the lives of all the children. In raising two children of my own and working with families, I have found children to be quite curious. They may have questions they want to ask you but are afraid to ask. When you are talking with the siblings of the ill child, allow them ample time to ask questions. Having an ill member of the family close in age to them can be overwhelming and somewhat frightening. Don't be surprised if other children ask if they could also become ill like their brother or sister. This certainly was a question that came up with my two boys.

In almost all cases, the chronically ill child leaves the healthcare setting and the parents assume responsibility for provision of care for the child in the home. It is important that the family care giver not feel alienated from professional medical resources. Parents need to consider their own limitations before adding more caregiving responsibilities to their routines. This is when the parents need to take a good close look at their family routines and how they will manage the extra responsibilities of caregiving when the ill child returns to the home environment. The clinical social worker is a good healthcare professional to assist you with a smooth transition of what is needed when the ill child returns home. Hopefully, if in home healthcare is needed for your child from trained professionals, this service will be arranged before coming home. Those visiting nurses who came to my home to start IVs and check on both boys when they were ill were my lifeline to the doctors at the hospital. I can't imagine what we would have done without them.

What do I mean by sense of control in dealing with your child's illness? You may say that I really don't have any say so over what is happening to my child. Yes, I get that. I really get where you are coming from. However, at times you are going to have choices about when certain things related to aspects of your child's care will be done. For example, you can determine when appointments may need to be made, procedures scheduled or even surgery. You may be balancing work, other kids' schedules, family life etc. When you are able, make choices that help you keep things running smoothly for your child, for you, and your family. When I felt so out of control with what was happening with my child's changing healthcare needs any semblance of control over the smallest thing seemed to make me feel better. Creating some semblance of control over what was happening to my child and when it was happening seemed to have a large impact for me emotionally. You and the child's physician may even have far reaching choices to make about your child's care.

Another thing that helped me cope was my belief in a higher power. I realize that this is not for everyone. I truly understand this.

But it did help me with both of my boys' illnesses. I believe God gave us a mind and body to use to our fullest potential. But sometimes I needed a strength beyond myself. I often reminded myself of one scripture when I would start to get anxious about the next day in my journey in raising two children with medical problems. That scripture referenced not worrying about tomorrow for tomorrow has enough trouble of its own. I would stay as much as I could in the present, the here and now. I would make the necessary provisions my child needed for his future, but I focused as much as possible on what was going on in the present.

Was it helpful for me to have all the medical and psychological knowledge I had in raising both my children with health problems? I would say both yes and no. It made me be a more educated advocate for my child, but it also let me know all too keenly what potential problems could become real possibilities. For me, this was why it was so important to stay focused on the present situation we were facing and not let my mind wander too far into the future. This is something I actively worked on in my personal coping. I stayed as much in the here and now as possible. At times I had to do a good bit of compartmentalizing to block out other extraneous stressful situations so I would not get too overwhelmed with my child's immediate health needs. Sometimes it was just too painful to attempt to predict my child's future. It was all I could do during the intense times of both children's illnesses just to manage the immediate day to day health care needs. But you know, as I reflect on all this, I somehow managed. So if I can manage, hopefully you can too.

Now that I have shared my story with each of you, I hope it was in some way helpful and encouraged you to stay strong and persevere through the difficult times your child may face.

CPSIA information can be obtained
at www.ICGtesting.com
Printed in the USA
FSHW012005250920
74097FS